INTO MUSIC

Book 3

PETER BROWN

Senior Music Lecturer
Bedford College of Physical Education

Consultant Editor
James Kirkpatrick

Head of Music
King Edward's School, Witley

Hulton Educational

Acknowledgement
The publishers are very grateful to Northern
Songs Ltd for allowing them to reproduce the
song 'When I'm Sixty-four' by Lennon and
McCartney

First published in Great Britain 1983
by Hulton Educational Publications Ltd
Raans Road, Amersham, Bucks HP6 6JJ

Text © Peter Brown 1983
Illustrations © Hulton Educational 1983

Edited and designed by James Shepherd
Artwork by Philip Schramm

ISBN 0 7175 1099 9

Text phototypeset by Input Typesetting Ltd, London
Music set by Collyer Graphics
Printed in Great Britain by The Pitman Press, Bath

Contents

1   THERE'S NO PLACE LIKE HOME

The degrees of a scale

Things to do

1. After each of the following pairs of phrases has been played on the piano, discuss which make a complete tune.

Compare the effect of reversing the phrases.

2. Send out volunteers. As each returns, they sing an 'answer' to the same sung or played 'question' phrase. Discuss the reason(s) if any sound unsatisfactory.

3. All sing a simultaneous 'answer' to another 'question'. Ignore the odd note mixtures and sing what first 'comes'. Was the last note agreed?

4. Sing the home note (doh) after each of these phrases is played. Do not look at the music:

Although major (and minor) key phrases may step or jump around:

and end on any note, a tune will not often sound finished unless its last phrase ends on a doh.

'There's no place like home'.

Nobody forgets where they live, so we can:
(a) Recognise when a tune finishes on a doh;
(b) Sing answering phrases that automatically end on doh;
(c) Sing doh when there is no doh in the tune.

Musicians normally use the following to describe the different steps (DEGREES) of each octave of any major or minor scale—whether singing or playing:

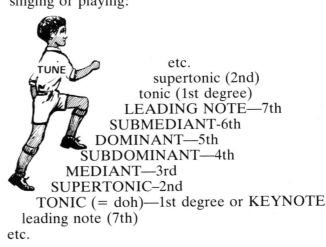

etc.
supertonic (2nd)
tonic (1st degree)
LEADING NOTE—7th
SUBMEDIANT-6th
DOMINANT—5th
SUBDOMINANT—4th
MEDIANT—3rd
SUPERTONIC–2nd
TONIC (= doh)—1st degree or KEYNOTE
leading note (7th)
etc.

In your music reading it is also time to stop the stage-by-stage introduction of the easier intervals. When singing, solfa was useful for this. These new names are certainly not meant to be sung—but there is nothing to stop singers from still 'thinking' solfa when working out intervals.

In your notebook

(i) (Copy, completing the words)
The ascending degrees of any major or minor scales are tonic, supertonic, ——, ——, ——, ——and——. The tonic is also called the——.

Things to do

5. Identify the intervals greater than a 5th in 1. Divide into two groups with chromatic instruments. One practise the first phrase of each tune, and the other the second. Join the phrases together, all playing just half the tune in the written order. Later, reverse the phrases.
6. Write the degrees of the scale corresponding to fah, lah, doh, soh, te, ray and me. What else is measured in degrees? Between which degrees is there a semitone? Suggest how the dominant, subdominant, leading note got their names.
7. Copy the following and write under each note its degree in the given major keys (scales):

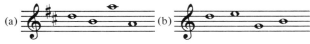
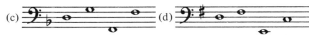

Now list the degrees of tune 1(c).
8. Use the correct clef and key signature writing the required degrees as semibreves at any 8ve:
(a) Treble stave, key F: dominant, mediant, subdominant;
(b) Bass stave, key C: tonic, submediant, leading note;
(c) Treble stave, key D: supertonic, dominant, keynote;
9. Write the required degrees as above, but do not use a key signature. Add accidentals:
(a) Treble stave, key G: mediant, leading note, tonic;
(b) Bass stave, key D; mediant, leading note, keynote;
(c) Treble stave, key F: dominant, subdominant, supertonic.

Tonic and dominant chords

Each degree can be the root of a chord (triad). Here are the chords built on each degree of the scale of C major. Chords may be named in several ways. For example, (a) after their root (C, G, etc.), or (b) by the position of their root in any key—

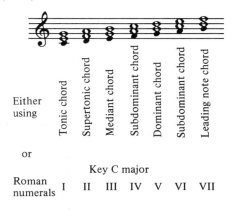

Either using	Tonic chord	Supertonic chord	Mediant chord	Subdominant chord	Dominant chord	Subdominant chord	Leading note chord
or							
			Key C major				
Roman numerals	I	II	III	IV	V	VI	VII

Things to do

10. Name the three scale degrees required for chord I. Which one is also in chord IV?
11. Copy the following, completing the Roman numerals under the triads for each key:

Key C: III V

Key G: VI I

12. Set out the following as in 11. Use the appropriate key signature on each treble stave:
(a) Key D: supertonic, leading note, dominant, mediant;
(b) Key F: leading note, tonic, subdominant, supertonic.
What do you notice about the first chord in 11(a), (b) and 12(a)? Discuss why the same chord can have different names. Why is the first chord of 12(b) not the same?

Within each key a chord has its own particular 'flavour'. The tonic chord (I) is the most important. Like the tonic note itself, the tonic chord has the 'home' flavour. Pieces therefore usually end on this chord.

The second most important chord (and note) is the dominant (V).

The dominant chord has an 'away' flavour. As it contains the leading note, it also usually suggests that it wants to go home to the tonic chord.

Chords are chosen to fit the notes of a tune. Much simple music can be harmonised using chords I and V. For example, 'London's burning':

Triads show the letters required by each chord. However, they would not normally be played as written. Chords can be spread out in many ways. Remember, the 'flavour' of a chord does not change when its notes

are rearranged

or have 'second helpings'.

The regular chord change pattern of 'London's burning' is unusual. Sometimes a chord lasts for several beats (or bars), especially when a phrase is the same broken chord. The melody notes change but the chord remains. For example, 'Clementine':

Sometimes chords have to change on successive notes (or beats), especially in music like hymns—and in 'Three blind mice':

Here are other songs that can be harmonised with just chords I and V:

'Polly Wolly Doodle'	'Down in the Valley'
'Bobby Shaftoe'	'The Yellow Rose of Texas'
'Clementine'	'One man went to mow'
'Michael Finnegan' 'My old man's a dustman'	'Skip to my Lou'

Things to do

13. First hear the chord of G played on the piano in the basic triad arrangement opposite. Then listen to various arrangements (with 'second helpings') of this chord. Similarly treat chord D. Get used to the 'home' and 'away' flavours of each when in key G. Now hear further versions of each one. Identify them as I (home) or V (away).

14. Listen to 'London's burning' harmonised as shown above. Repeat, with the harmony (a) all chord I, (b) all chord V, (c) the chords reversed. Discuss why (c) caused the most clashes.

15. Listen to the above songs played/sung and harmonised in key G with chord I only. Notice when the tune clearly has an 'argument' with the harmony. Repeat, this time with your eyes closed. Put your hand up and down each time you think the chord should change to V. Now hear them harmonised properly. Which two songs could fit against each other as they have the same time and harmony?

In your notebook

(ii) (Copy, unjumbling the words)
Chords are named after their *toros*. The most important and frequently used one is the *cinto* chord. Pieces end on this as it has the *meho* 'flavour'. The next most important chord is the *tin nomad*. This has an *yawa* 'flavour'.

Things to do

16. Repeat 13 in different keys.
17. Repeat 15, first in key C, then in F and D.

Changing key is rather like moving home. For a time, the new house may not feel right. For example,

what is 'away' in C is 'home' in G:

The new 'home' can feel 'away' for a while!

Remember to state the key when describing chords as tonic/I, etc.—otherwise it's like writing a number but no street name on an envelope!

Things to do

18. Recognise chords I and V in key G as in 13. Follow this by hearing chords I and V in key C played *once*. Continue I/V recognition in the new key. Why may you be confused at first?
19. Repeat 18, recognising tonic and dominant *notes*, not chords. Is there the same confusion?
20. You do not need the gift of absolute pitch to remember keys for a while. Listen to 'London's burning' in one key and then in others. Recognise when the original key returns.
21. Sing 'London's burning' in key A. Why are some notes 'black'. Do they sound 'black'?

Key A major

A major needs three 'black' notes to make the correct track of

tones and semitones:

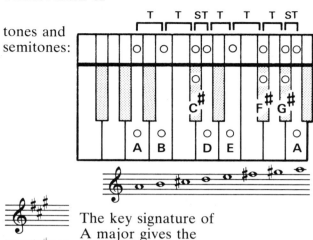

The key signature of A major gives the three sharps required.

The following song is in A major. It also only requires chords I and V in its accompaniment:

The chord letters, written above the tune, are placed either at every chord change or at every bar. See how most parts fit A(C# E) or E(G# B).

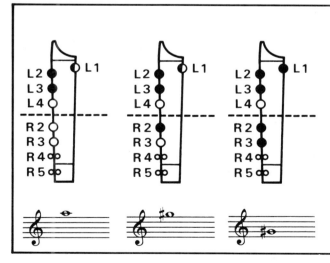

Here are the new recorder notes required to play in the key of A major. Again, the fingering for the pinched upper octave matches, or nearly matches, the lower octave. (What rule seems to be followed?) First practise changing octave between the two As and G#s. Next, practise the A major scale up and down.

The bass part requires an E. The cello D string will have to be stopped to get it. Similar stops are required in later parts.

Bass parts may be played on large glockenspiels, etc. (ignore rests) or sung by broken

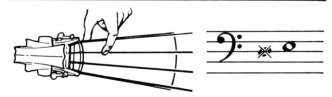

voices ('la', etc.) Many men are not true basses/tenors. Instead they have middle-range BARITONE voices. Similarly, many girls/ladies are MEZZO ('metso') SOPRANOS. A few men develop a treble range voice as well (MALE ALTO/COUNTER TENOR).

Things to do

22. First play A major scales on any chromatic class instruments. Identify the 6th jumps in the song and first part. Take turns at accompanying and/or playing the song. Add a chorus 'fa la'.

A Scottish student song: **'The Spanish Guitar'**

2 HARMONY IN THE HOME

Playing chords

Most instruments cannot play chords on their own. However, all those instruments that can only sound one note at a time can help to make up a chord—as in the last song accompaniment. The composer or arranger has to see that the parts added together make the chords required:

You played chords together like this in the last song. For example, the accompaniment of the first complete bar adds up to chord A(C# E).

DIY chords are also possible. For example:
(a) Divide the class into groups (rows, tables, etc.) according to the number of chords required. The members of each group contribute just one note to their chord:

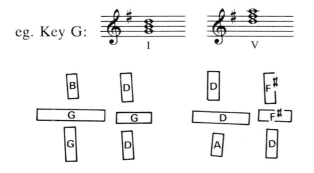

Notice that the same note can belong to two (or more) chords. Notice also that different 8ves and 'second helpings' are possible.

(b) Each person has just one note. It is played (P) only when it fits the chord required:

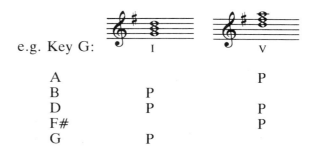

e.g. Key G:	I	V
A		P
B	P	
D	P	P
F#		P
G	P	

(c) Each person has note(s) to contribute to each of the chords:

D—	D	D
GA	G	A
BD	B	D
GF#	G	F#

Class instruments such as chime bars and glockenspiels (diatonic or chromatic as required) would be the most appropriate. The piano, recorders and orchestral instruments could also be used. The root of each chord can be plucked on the cello/bass (especially if an open string) or played on a low-pitched class instrument/piano.

Several playing styles are possible with these methods:
(i) Play a sustained note at each chord change.
(ii) Play at the beginning of each bar, repeating the same notes if the chord is the same.
(iii) As (ii) but playing an ostinato rhythm appropriate for the time, e.g.

Damp when necessary. (ii) and (iii) will not work if there is more than one chord in a bar.

Things to do

1. Assemble instruments to play chords I (tonic) and V (dominant) in key G. Suggest why it is more helpful for players to refer to these chords as G(BD) and D(F# A).

Now accompany 'London's burning' (page 6) played on the piano using the above methods (a), (b) and (c) in turn. Play at each chord change (style (i)).

2. Use one of the methods to accompany a group singing/playing the song (i) in unison, (ii) as a round with one-bar delay.

Can you now see why the chords are so regular?

3. Choose one of the songs on page 6, repeating Chapter 1, 15 in key G.

With the words written on the board, add G (home) and D (away) under them at each chord change. Work out its time and choose playing style (i), (ii) or (iii) as appropriate. At first, just play the chord roots as an accompaniment. When this is satisfactory, play the full chords in three ways as in 1 above.

4. Privately practise playing the above song on any available instrument. Play by 'ear', remembering that it may not begin on the tonic. If it goes too high or low for your instrument, start at a different octave. When ready, play to the class, others singing if the key is suitable.

Finally, accompany a group playing/singing the tune with the chords.

5. Repeat 3 and 4 with other page 6 songs, but without the words or chords written down.

6. Repeat 1–5 in key A.

Chord instruments

Some instruments can, of course, play chords on their own. In addition to the normal keyboard family you can all use the following:

Melodica

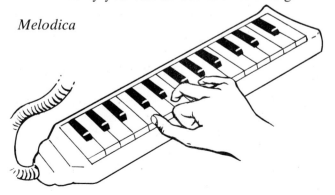

Use a stand for the best 'visibility'. In addition to single notes in methods (a), (b) and (c), one or more triads may be fingered or tongued in an appropriate rhythm: e.g.

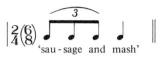

Autoharp

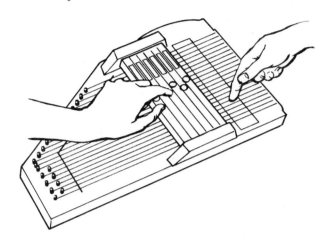

Strum the required chords. The chord roots are shown on the damping bars.

This is also a good time to start learning the most popular chord-playing instrument. In any case, it will be useful to know a little more about it. There are several types, including:

Spanish (classical) guitar (gut or nylon strings)   Flat top (folk/ acoustic) guitar (steel strings)   Solid electric guitar (steel strings)

Although tunes can be played in the Spanish style, most people use the guitar to play chords. The notes may be strummed or picked in succession. As the six open strings (numbered as shown) do not make a triad,

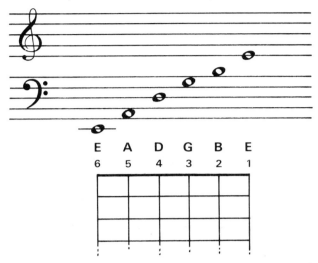

one or more of them have to be stopped for each chord:

Pressing a finger behind a fret, e.g.:

shortens the vibrating length of the string. Each fret makes the string's pitch a semitone higher:

(E string)

F 1st fret

(F♯) 2nd fret

(G) 3rd fret

Although guitarists can play from normal music, chords are usually read from string/fingering diagrams (tablature), as with the lute.

Here is one way of fingering chord C:

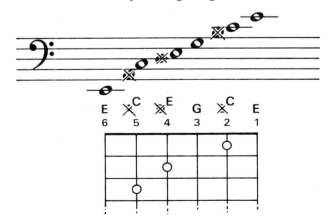

If you have a guitar, there are easy ways of playing two chords. First tune the strings as above. Then get into the playing position:

The fingers are numbered. Unlike recorder players and pianists, guitarists do not count the thumb.

Chord diagrams show:
(a) Where any strings have to be stopped;
(b) Which LH fingers to use;
(c) The strings to be plucked/strummed (bracketed).
  Now practise the following three-string chords. See that the last finger joint is square to the strings. Strum downwards with the RH thumb:

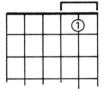 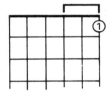

Key C: 'home' (I)   'away' (V)

First, name the letters sounded in V. Explain why the wrong note does not clash.
Change chord, playing four strums on each. indicates a beginner guitar (ukelele/banjo) activity.
  At present, strum on every beat or just once at each chord change. You could even change fixed-fingered guitarists instead of changing chords!

Things to do

7. Identify pegs, fingerboard, bridge, frets on the guitar pictures and available instruments. Discuss (a) differences between types, (b) why the autoharp is like a mechanical guitar.
8. Draw a six-string diagram for chord G.
9. Compare the guitar, violin and bass open string intervals. Why is the guitar's 'lowest' string also the highest?

3 WHAT'S THE SCORE?

The dominant seventh

The following aria (song) from a Classical comic opera also only requires chords I and V in the accompaniment. It was an immediate hit. Wherever Mozart's opera was performed this tune caught on like wildfire—even without the help of records and radio. A young page (Cherubino) has to join his master's regiment. In the song, a servant (Figaro) humorously reminds him of what he is going to miss.

(a) Listen to a recording of this song. It will probably be sung in the original Italian. Many composers at this time considered it fashionable to write operas in Italian—whatever their nationality. What voice sings Figaro?

Follow it through three verses, each separated by a section of recitative warning Cherubino of the dangers of war. The final coda is also based just on chords I and V.

Discuss how Mozart suggests war in both the melody and the accompaniment.

A song from *The Marriage of Figaro*: 'Say goodbye now'   **Mozart**

Things to do

1. Assemble instruments to play chords C and G as in Chapter 2. A group accompany the singing of the song, Use methods (a), (b) or (c), playing either at each chord change or repeating the chord at each bracket as well. Later, include a few players on the tune as well. Why is the tune so jumpy?

2. If suitable instruments are available, add bass notes (a) to the above ensemble. Use tenor/bass class instruments/cello open strings. Play at each letter indication. Boys with broken voices could also sing in the song's rhythm at higher 8ves (b):

3. Look at the above melody. Collect all the notes accompanied by chord C, writing each new one on the treble stave as a chord. Here are the first two:

Include different 8ves, but not 'second helpings' of the same 8ve. Do they all belong to the C triad? Repeat with the notes accompanied by chord G. Discuss (a) extra, (b) missing notes?

4. Now non-guitarists study the chord V diagram on page 11. Work out the letters sounded on the three bracketed strings. Try to explain any wrong note.

12

The triad pattern can be extended by at least one further 3rd:

The extra note is a 7th above the root

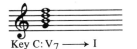

This happens most frequently with chord V.

The above chord is therefore called G₇ or the DOMINANT SEVENTH (V₇) of Key C:

Key C: V₇ ⟶ I   The extra note strengthens the 'going home' effect.

This explains why there are Fs in (a) the song's G chord sections, (b) guitar chord V on page 11, and Ds in the E chord sections of the page 8 song.

Beginner guitarists can now learn to play chords C and G₇ the proper way. First practise them separately, repeatedly strumming the indicated strings. Notice (a) finger 1 is used as in the easy three-string versions, (b) the chords have a similar pattern.

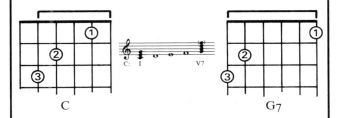

C   G₇

Next, practise changing between them, strumming four times on each. Try to move all the fingers at once—not one at a time. You should aim to do this without having to look.

Now repeat previous key C two-chord accompaniments (including the song on page 12). Also join in the following activities using these chords. Use G₇ when G is indicated. In any key, V₇ can always be used instead of V.

Two-chord tunes

Chords are chosen to match the tune. The reverse is also possible. You are now going to compose tunes to match the notes of a chord. Triad notes and 7ths can be used at any 8ve.

Things to do

5. Compare chords V and V₇ in key C, both played on a piano in various arrangements (a) on their own, (b) followed each time by chord I. Although the basic chord flavour is unchanged, the 'going home' effect is strengthened by the 7th.

6. Sing 'One man went to mow' or 'My old man's a dustman' (key C), adding an accompaniment as before. This time you may add the 7th to the dominant. Both have the same chord plan:

Now write your own tune to fit these chords. Keep the time the same and use this rhythm:

Use only chord notes and no leger lines other than middle C. Do not jump more than an octave, and end on the tonic note. Listen to each tune played with the correct accompaniment. Vote for the best. Notice any tune notes that clash with the chord. A group play the winning tune on any suitable instrument(s). Accompany with the chords played as before.

7. Learn to play your tune on an instrument of your choice. Take turns at playing to the class. Now, all play your tunes simultaneously. Why should they mix so well? Finally, mix some of your tunes as an accompaniment for the above two songs sung together by two small groups.

8. Make up words (one or more verses) for either (a) the winning tune, (b) your tune. Accented syllables should always be on beat one. Again vote for the best and combine.

9. Write another tune to the above chord plan, but this time in key G. Change also to 3/4 time and make up your own rhythm. End each phrase on a long note and otherwise keep to the previous instructions. Perform and accompany as in the above. Later, similarly compose tunes in any time in keys, D, A and F. Work out the chord notes first.

The orchestral score

It is not only simple songs that can be based on chords I and V. Many Classical instrumental movements, like the following, begin thus.

Although the most important composers in the Classical Period were Austrian/German, the instruments, tempo, words and other instructions are usually in Italian. Even today, many composers still keep to this language.

 (b) Listen just to the Andante section. As you follow the music, do not count beats to keep your place. Neither try to follow eleven staves at once! Instead:

(i) Notice the first loud tutti (full orchestra);

(ii) Follow the soft 1st oboe melody up a broken chord and down a scale. Notice when the bassoons and 2nd oboe start accompanying.

(iii) Look ahead for another loud tutti chord;

(iv) Again follow the 1st oboe up and down. Then immediately look down the score for:

(v) Descending staccato low string notes.

(vi) A two-bar violin stepping phrase (doubled by the bassoons). Get ready for:

(vii) Five final loud tutti chords. Notice that they are separated by rests in the strings, but joined (legato) in the wind.

The opening of the Overture to *Cosi Fan Tutti*, K.588   Mozart

Orchestral scores are arranged down the page, with the woodwind, brass, percussion and strings each bracketed, in descending pitch order. In the Classical orchestra, two players are usually required for each wind and brass instrument. The 1st and 2nd players take the upper and lower notes respectively. The cello and bass often share the same stave.

The first line shows all the instruments required. After this most printers omit the staves of those instruments not playing—and also give only instrument abbreviations. Although reduced scores are separated by ⸓ , this can be confusing. One expects the top stave always to be the flute!

In your notebook

(i) (Copy, completing the words)
In an orchestral score, the woodwind staves are at the top, followed by ——, —— and —— staves. Each family of instruments is —— together, in —— pitch order.

Things to do

10. Assemble fading-sound instruments to play chords I (C) and V₇ (G₇) in key C. If necessary/possible, tune the recording by adjusting its speed. Now, play the appropriate chord at the beginning, and at each chord change, with the first eight bars of the recording. Notice how both the orchestral chords and tune fit against your harmony. Compare this chord pattern with that of the two songs in 6. Finally, discuss the time of this overture.

11. Now hear the Andante and the beginning of the next section. Beat four crotchets in a bar. Is it a problem changing speed at the presto?

C and ¢ time

At fast speeds beating gets awkward!

When crotchet beats are too fast to beat comfortably:
Minim beats at half the speed may be beaten instead:

So, the beat unit need not always be the ♩ (or ♩.).

The lower figure of the time signature gives the value (American name) of the beat unit used.

In the overture, instead of:

Four **4** there are Two **2**
Crotchet **4** beats Minim **2** beats
in a bar in a bar

These time signatures are often replaced by:

C ¢

(See the page 12 song) and (See page 14)

These signs originated in the Middle Ages when time signatures were based on complete or broken circles (O C). Today, printers make the second sign look like the letter C. However, this is not the reason why 4/4 may be called 'common time'. It just happens to be a commonly used time.

In the overture, Mozart perhaps should have written **C** for the andante and ¢ for the presto.

Many pieces with a time signature of 4/4 (**C**) may be treated as if they were in 2/2 (¢). It depends on how fast they are performed.

Fast beats are not only uncomfortable for conductors, they hinder a flowing style of performance. Consider 'Good King Wenceslas':

In his Mas-ter's steps he trod,

At slower tempi, the beat should obey the time signature, and walk in step with the page. At faster tempi, it would be more musical to beat minims and walk more slowly in step with the king. Notice that although the page's feet (crotchets) go twice as fast as the king's (minims), both characters (the music) move forward at the same speed.

Things to do

12. Listen twice more to the Mozart extract. Compare the effect as you beat (a) 4/4 time, (b) 2/2 time during both sections.
13. Sing 'Good King Wenceslas' at a slow tempo, simultaneously beating 'in step with the page' (4/4 time). Repeat, each time at a faster tempo. When four beats in a bar is uncomfortably fast, change gear to be 'in step with the king' (2/2 time). Now, at this same tempo, divide into two singing groups. One group beat 4/4 (or mark time) and the other 2/2. Notice that changing gear need not change the actual speed of the notes performed.
14. Turn to page 14. Write out the 1st bassoon part of bars 10 and 11 on the treble stave. Compare with the 1st violin part. Work out the interval between (a) the viola and cello parts in bars 12–14, (b) the violin parts in bars 19–23.

In your notebook

(ii) (Copy, completing the words)
The lower figure of the t——s—— gives the American name of the beat unit. C may be used instead of 4/4 or c—— time, and ₵ instead of 2/2 time.

Sonata form

The main presto section of the Overture to *Cosi Fan Tutti* is in SONATA FORM. This was the most important musical 'recipe' invented by the classical composers. As it was particularly used in the first movements of their instrumental works, it is also known as FIRST MOVEMENT FORM.

Sonata form is not an exact recipe. No two musical 'cooks' make it the same way. As a rough guide, two sorts of things usually happen:

(a) Various themes/musical ideas/subjects are introduced. These (or parts of them called 'figures'/motifs) are then played around with in any way the composer likes. They usually return in their original form at the end.
(b) After starting in the TONIC KEY, the music modulates to other major and minor keys. It usually returns to the original (tonic) key at the end.

You must not expect musical subjects always to be complete tunes. Often they are just easily remembered melodic or rhythmic starting points. Although not complete in themselves, they are useful for future 'discussion'.

Also, do not confuse sonata *form* with its ensemble meaning. Remember, one or more movements of a piano *sonata* may be in sonata *form*—but so may an overture, and the movements of a symphony, concerto or quartet, etc. Some composers still use sonata form today.

The first and last movement of a work, but not necessarily the others, are normally in the same (tonic) key. This is the key of the work as a whole.

(c) Turn to the music on page 14. First get used to the reduced scores, the use of // and the abbreviations of the Italian instrument names. Next, make yourselves familiar with presto themes/musical ideas V, W, X, Y and Z. Now listen to the complete overture. Count two beats in a bar as you follow the printed extract. Notice:
(i) The 2nd violins join the 1sts after V;
(ii) The loud tutti chords of W;
(iii) Wind imitation using X, followed by a drum roll and the return of:
(iv) V, in imitation, and in another key;
(v) W again, also in a different key;
(vi) Y on the high woodwind combined with Z on the violins.

As the music continues, you will notice at various times, the return of each of these themes/ideas:
Changes of key (modulations)
More imitation
A return to the tonic key at the end
Final repetitions of the tonic chord.
Finally, (vii) discuss which of the above are 'themes' and which 'musical ideas', (vii) what 'a 2' means (bar 25), (ix) how ♪ is played (bar 45).

4 NOT WHAT IT SEEMS

The Classical orchestra

The picture below shows the standard Classical orchestra. When accompanying an opera, it would be placed low down in the pit, between the audience and the stage. It is the line-up required for Mozart's *Cosi Fan Tutti*—and for most symphonies and concerto accompaniments of the period. The overture to this opera, like many others, is often played as a separate concert item.

Unlike the other instrumental families, the number of string players is not fixed. In this picture, both 1st and 2nd violins are to the left of the conductor. Sometimes they are on either side of him. The orchestral leader always sits at the front, to the left of the conductor. When two players share a music stand (DESK), the rear string player and 2nd player of other instruments turn over the music.

Things to do

1. The instruments shown in the score on page 14 are all in the above picture. Identify (a) each one, (b) the leader. Which family has the (c) biggest, (d) smallest membership in this orchestra? Each family except the strings is a mixed consort. What does this mean? Why do you think the recorder consort is not used in an orchestra? Which two Italian instrument names would you have guessed were different instruments? Why is an opera orchestra put in a pit?

2. Draw a rough layout plan of the orchestra. Just show the general position of each family. Suggest why certain instruments are placed at the back.

3. Again look at the score (page 14). In the extract, which instruments have (a) the smallest, (b) the largest total number of bars rest, (c) the longest single rest period?

Long rests

In an orchestra, or any other ensemble, nobody plays all the time. Brass and percussion players usually have the longest rests. String players are normally the hardest worked. It can be embarrassing for a person who has to play loudly after a long rest!

Here is a safe counting method:

1 2 3 4 **2** 2 3 4 **3** 2 3 4 etc.

Only the conductor reads from a score. The players just have their parts. Imagine cutting out the timpani part and pasting the strips below each other. A lot of space would be wasted on rests.

To prevent this, long rests are written differently. For example, on page 14, the flutes' second long rest would look like this:

On each part is printed the same bar numbers and playing information as on the score. This aids both rehearsal and performance.

Things to do

4. Write out the second clarinet and timpani parts of the Mozart overture (pages 14, 15) to bar 29. Use long rests and add all the performing instructions. Suggest (a) Why the timpani are tuned to C and G in this work;
(b) Why the brass and timpani parts usually have the most rests;
(c) One disadvantage for the player of not being able to see the other parts. Now discuss:
(d) What orchestral players should be doing during 'rests';
(e) Whether the music stops when everybody has a rest (e.g. bar 1 of music, page 14).
5. Here is a test of nerve. First practise saying the following words in the given rhythm. Now all count the fourteen bars' rest silently at the same tempo, saying the words very loudly when you come to them.

Alternatively, you could be accompanied by a sixteen-bar 4/4 piano piece:

'This is the end'

6. Assemble chime bars to play one octave of a D major scale (with 'second helpings' but no different 8ves, except D). Each take one bar and beater. Now turn to Chapter 1, 1(a), noting when your bar is used. Now write a part for it. Use crotchet ₹ , single bar ▬ and long rests only.

For example, G would begin:

Finally, all play (and damp) your parts simultaneously. Melody (a) should result.

7. Each choose any unpitched or single note (of a) pitched instrument. Write a sixteen-bar 3/4 part for it on a single-line stave as in 5 (whether pitched or unpitched). Use just a few notes and many rests and add dynamics as in this example:

All play simultaneously under a conductor. Later, change instruments or parts. Will you expect any chords to be triads?
8. Repeat 7, with each final bar:

9. Practise each of the following parts, saying (and sustaining) the words in the given rhythm:

When perfect, combine them in three groups under a conductor. Suggest why writing the above parts as a score would have given the game away. Record and play back your performance.

Syncopation

(a) Listen again to bars 15–60 (pages 14–15). Beat 2/2 time as you look at the music. Notice an interesting rhythmic effect in each W section. A similar thing occurs in the woodwind in each Y section. Discuss what happens.

Here is the first bar rhythm of W as 'sausages on sticks': the longer note begins between the beats:

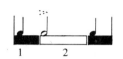

As longer notes *appear* louder than shorter ones, there is the effect of an off-beat accent.

The woodwind rhythm throughout Y is very similar: Notice, two tied crotchets equal one minim: off-beat (or weak beat) accents also seem to occur when there is a rest on the previous beat, or because of a rest or tie, no note

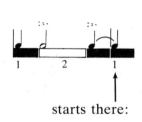

starts there:

It is normal for any accents to occur on the beats, especially the first in each bar. SYNCOPATION occurs with off-beat accents.
And when weaker beats are deliberately accented by adding a real accent:
or a dynamic mark such as *sf*
Not only jazz and pop are SYNCOPATED:

Opening of Minuet (and Trio):
Symphony No. 40   **Mozart**

(b) Listen to the above Minuet and Trio, following the extract each time it occurs in a recording. Beat time, noticing the effect of the ties. Which movement would this be?
(c) Hear examples of jazz/pop syncopation. Clap/play a tambourine (a) on, (b) off the main beats.

(d) Listen to the third movement of Beethoven's Violin Sonata in F Major, Op. 24 ('Spring'). Continuous syncopation is unusual—try to beat time! Is the form large-scale binary (AB) or ternary (ABA)? Identify A 'crumbs' in the B section.

Beethoven called the above movement a SCHERZO (Italian for 'joke'). The lively scherzo had begun to replace the Minuet and Trio in the third movement spot. A contrasting middle section (also often called a trio) gives the scherzo the same overall ternary plan.

Things to do

10. Compare the rhythm of the Mozart extract clapped/played on class instruments/piano (a) ignoring ties, (b) correctly, with syncopation.
11. List the letter names played in bar 5, beat 1 on page 14. Are the horns 'wrong'?

Instruments that transpose

Some instruments do not sound the notes read by the player. There are reasons for this:
(a) Very high-pitched instruments like the piccolo and descant recorder are written an 8ve lower than they sound. This reduces the leger lines:

(b) The low-pitched double bass is similarly written an 8ve higher than it sounds.
8(8ve) and 8ve basso respectively show that all is 'not what it seems'.
(c) Some instruments, like the clarinet, horn and trumpet, come in different sizes (or have different extension crooks to lower their register). This could cause players a problem. With each increasing size (or crook) lower notes are produced by the same fingering! (And the same notes require different fingerings.)

On the true note (C) version Middle C fingering produces:
But on B♭ versions, Middle C fingering produces B♭—a tone *lower*:

So, if the composer really wants C to sound, he has to write a tone *higher* as a tone *lower* is sounded.

With larger sizes, the player just pretends he has the C version. The composer ensures that written notes are always fingered the same. E.g. the horns used on page 14 are in G. This means that Middle C fingering produces:

As all the notes will sound an interval of a 4th *lower*, Mozart had to write every horn note a 4th *higher* than the one he really wanted.

Instruments that 'do not speak the truth' (including those written an 8ve higher or lower) are called TRANSPOSING INSTRUMENTS.

For this piece, Mozart requires CONCERT PITCH(C) clarinets and trumpets. Today, versions in B^b or A are usually used.

Several recorders are transposing instruments. Here is the basic two-octave compass of each one. The same fingering produces alternately the C and F major scales:

There are also two other rarely used sizes:
Sopranino; sounding an 8ve above the treble.
Double bass; sounding an 8ve below the tenor.

Some descant players could now transfer to the treble or tenor recorders. Most solos have been written for the mellow-toned treble.

Use the tenor to play all descant music, as the fingering and *written* notes are the same.

The treble recorder would also be no problem if it was treated like a transposing instrument. With its part written a 4th lower than required, you could pretend it was a descant! Unfortunately, treble players must eventually get used to the C scale fingering while looking at F scale notes.

First get used to the size of any new instruments. Tenor players practise the scales of C, D, F, G and A.

Treble players practise the scales of F, G and D using the descant fingerings for C, D and A, and play known tunes by 'ear' using descant fingering. Discuss why you may not look at any music yet.

Descant (and tenor) players now practise the above scales up and down in different rhythms. (a) Tongue separately, (b) slur pairs of notes, (c) slur the scale.

Now compare any pitch on the descant with the piano and/or treble/tenor recorders. Can you tell you have not been 'speaking the truth'? Discuss why the treble compass looks higher than the descant's.

 (d) Hear music from different periods featuring the various recorders.
(e) Listen to short extracts and match with a word from each column. Discuss identifying 'fingerprints':

Period	Composer	Type of work
Early Baroque	Handel	madrigal
Classical	Purcell	symphony
Renaissance	Beethoven	trio sonata
Late Baroque	Thomas Morley	early opera

Things to do

12. Repeat 11, but writing the notes *sounded* on the treble and bass staves. Repeat 8ves, but ignore 'second helpings'. Take account of transposing instruments. What is the chord?
13. Write out the letters sounded by a treble recorder when a descant C scale is fingered.
14. Hear transposing instruments play a given note. Let the piano prove the 'lie'.
15. Use the part written in 4 to 'play' timpani (real/imagined) with a recording.

5 THE ROMANTIC PERIOD

ROMANTIC is the name given to the music, art and literature of the nineteenth century. The word has no special connection with to-day's meaning of 'romance'. After all, musicians, painters and poets of many periods naturally have a special interest in the 'boy meets girl' theme. A romantic view of life means many other things as well. The most important of these is that the individual is free to express his or her imagination and emotions in any way. For the composer, this means writing what he likes when he wants to. Fortunately, from Beethoven onwards most of them were free to do just this. In keeping with the revolutionary spirit of the times, artists generally had freed themselves from the service of kings, local rulers and the Church. Unfortunately, artists were also now free to starve— especially if they had no patron to support them. Instead of writing large numbers of works to order, whatever their mood, they now wrote for the new prosperous middle-class audiences.

For many ordinary people, however, the nineteenth century was hardly 'romantic'—in any sense. It began with the French Revolution, Napoleon, Wellington, Nelson and many battles. Press gangs abducted men into the navy, and life could be squalid, especially in the towns. In the factories that sprang up during the Industrial Revolution, working conditions were hard. Workers were often little better than slaves.

In Britain, poverty was often treated as a crime. The workhouse, and even transportation for stealing a loaf of bread, were the fate of many.

Nineteenth-century music

The Romantic Period at first brought no great change in musical fashions. Composers just let themselves go more, and worried less about the musical form they were using. Self-expression

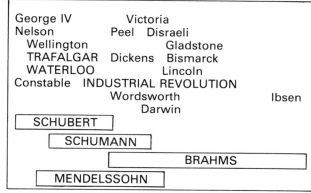

1600	1700	1800	1900

George IV   Victoria
Nelson   Peel Disraeli
  Wellington   Gladstone
  TRAFALGAR Dickens Bismarck
  WATERLOO   Lincoln
Constable INDUSTRIAL REVOLUTION
          Wordsworth   Ibsen
            Darwin

SCHUBERT
  SCHUMANN
          BRAHMS
  MENDELSSOHN

led to greater contrasts. Loud and soft, fast and slow became more extreme, and the musical expression of happiness and sorrow more exaggerated—minor keys and richer chords becoming more common. Works became longer, and larger orchestras, choirs and new instruments were often required. It was also the age of the VIRTUOSO player—who was often also a composer for his instrument.

Unlike previous periods, there was now no common style among composers. Everybody did their own thing—and several specialised in just one or two types of music. For this reason, you cannot recognise Romantic music in a quiz in the same way as, e.g. Classical music. Instead, it is particular composers that can be recognised—or their nationality.

Nationalism

In the nineteenth century, German supremacy in music began to be challenged. Also, several countries came on the scene for the first time. Proud of making the grade, Frederyk Chopin (Poland), Peter Tchaikovsky (Russia), Bedrich Smetana and Anton Dvorak (Bohemia), Edvard Grieg (Norway) and other NATIONALISTIC composers often included the rhythms and styles of their native folk music in their works.

Programme music

Composers not only wrote longer examples of the classical forms. New types of works appeared. In particular, they introduced TONE (SYMPHONIC) POEMS. In these pieces they tried to suggest something else behind the music (PROGRAMME MUSIC instead of ABSOLUTE MUSIC). Stories or titles such as 'Nightingale', 'Evening' or 'Sea' suggest the picture the listeners should have in mind. Several composers wrote BALLET music. As it illustrates a story in dance, ballet is a form of programme music. Tone poems were written by Franz Liszt (Hungary), who was also a virtuoso pianist,

Hector Berlioz (France), Richard Strauss (Germany) and a number of the Nationalist composers. Tchaikovsky (Russia) is particularly famous for his ballets.

However, the most important symphony, concerto and chamber music composers were still Austro-German.

23

Franz Schubert

Born in Vienna in 1797, Franz was another child prodigy from a musical family—the thirteenth of fourteen children! Whenever he saw the older Beethoven in a Viennese restaurant, he was too shy to speak! He also wrote hundreds of songs, known by the German name of LIEDER (pron. 'leader'). He died penniless at 32 from typhus, never hearing his last works.

Robert Schumann

Born in 1810, Robert also showed early musical genius, but first studied law in Leipzig. He married Clara, the daughter of his piano teacher there—after much objection from the father. He, too, wrote many lieder. Other compositions include many short piano pieces reflecting his split personality. The contrasting impulsive and dreamy sides to his nature he named Florestan and Eusebius. Always unstable, he died in a mental home in 1856.

Felix Mendelssohn

One of the few composers born in a rich family (to a Hamburg banker in 1809), Felix had music publicly performed when only ten. He was one of the first specialist conductors, introducing the music of Bach during his many visits to Britain. He died young in 1847.

Johannes Brahms

Also born in Hamburg, in 1833, Brahms later became a great friend of the Schumanns. His symphonies are the greatest since Beethoven. He died in Vienna in 1897.

Later in the century, Anton Bruckner and Gustav Mahler continued the German symphonic tradition. Another German, Richard Wagner, wrote very great (and very long) operas. However, Italy was (and is) the great opera-loving country. Guiseppe Verdi and others produced many works perfectly suited to the emotional singing appreciated by the Italians.

Later, composers such as Claude Debussy and Maurice Ravel (France) bring us into the twentieth century with new scales/harmony.

 Hear examples of Romantic music.

In your notebook

(i) Write a few sentences under (a) Romanticism, (b) Nationalism, (c) Programme Music.

Assignments

(A) Find out what the non-musicians on the above chart are famous for.
(B) List musicians/non-musicians who could have been included on it.
(C) Use the above information to write about life in the nineteenth century.

6 JUST PERFECT!

Polonaise and Mazurka

The next piece is a fine example of Romantic emotional music and of Nationalism. Frederyk Chopin was born in Poland of a French mother and Polish father. Although he settled in Paris, he was proud of his homeland and often introduced Polish dance rhythms in his music. These include the triple-time MAZURKA and POLONAISE. Chopin is also an example both of the virtuoso and of the specialist composer. Nearly all his works are for the piano.

Here is the complete plan of the piece, showing how the extracts (shaded) fit into each section:

A	:	a	A	:
B	:	b	B	:
A		a	A	

(a) Follow the RH tune in the two extracts. In A notice:
(i) The initial repeated A major tonic chord;
(ii) A rich and unusual chord at W.
(iii) A modulation, and then a return to A major.
In B notice:
(iv) The new key signature. What key is it?
(v) The typical polonaise rhythm in the LH.
(vi) Where the RH tune is at X.
(vii) Chromatic scales in contrary 8ves at Y.
(viii) A sudden key change at Z.

Extracts from: Polonaise in A major, Op. 40, No. 1   **Chopin**

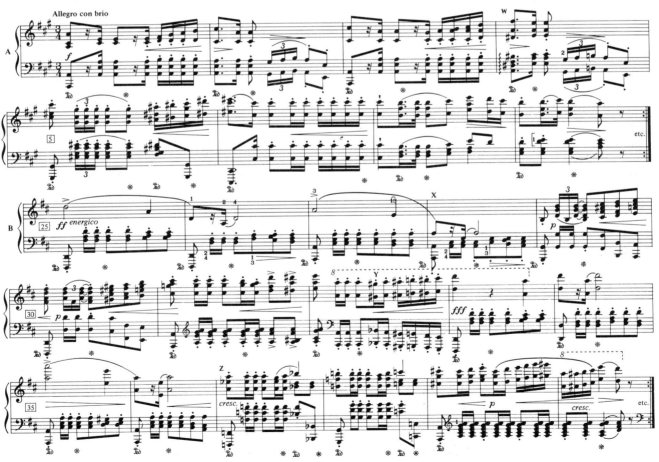

(b) Listen to the whole work. Follow the extracts each time they occur. Now discuss (ix) the form of the A and B sections, taken separately, (x) the form of the polonaise as a whole, (xi) what all the Italian words and abbreviations mean, (xii) what 8--- means at Y, (xiii) what makes it difficult to play.
(c) Listen to a Chopin Mazurka: the RH will have the tune, and the LH the accompaniment.

Things to do

1. Beat time while the above polonaise is played again. Notice how many phrases end (or accents occur) on the 2nd beat. Repeat with the mazurka, again noticing syncopated rhythms.
2. Accompany the polonaise with a group playing the LH rhythm of bar 25 as an ostinato.

It was through the polonaise in particular that Chopin expressed the heroism of the Polish people, and their constant struggle against oppression. Like most of Chopin's piano pieces, our example is in ternary form. The tonic key of its B section is D major. The new key signature saves having to naturalise the Gs.

The quick jumpy fat chords and the 8ves in both hands make the piece difficult—large hands might be an advantage!

Good pianists, like organists, also have to play with their feet. For example, look at bars 1 to 4 of the B extract. Chopin wants the low bass note at the beginning of each bar to mix with the jumpy chords that follow. The player therefore depresses the R (sustaining) pedal so that the notes continue sounding even after the keys come up. It is also important that the pedal comes up at the correct place. Bad pianists keep their feet down too long and mix chords together.

The timing of piano (R) pedalling is shown by

$$\text{𝄢𝅘} \qquad \text{❋}$$

or   P‿‿‿‿‿‿⌐‿‿‿⌐

Waltz and Study

The following WALTZ by Chopin shows his usual style—a RH tune with the LH chords arranged as an 'um pah pah'. Note the pedal timing. Chopin often has just one chord in a bar.

(d) Listen to this waltz. Notice (i) the introductory four-bar 'warm up', (ii) the rushing RH tune with its LH 'um pah pah', (iii) a contrasting middle section with RH tune in longer notes but with the same LH accompaniment, (iv) a return to the rushing tune, (v) a final presto descending scale. Do you know this piece's nickname? Is it a sensible one? What is the form of this waltz?

Things to do

3. Look at the given music. The opening harmony is very simple as the chords change between I and V every four bars. Listen to (a) the LH alone played slowly and with the pedal held down all the time, (b) as (a) but with each four-bar section pedalled together, (c) as (b) but with the RH added. Discuss (i) why (a) is unsatisfactory, (ii) why (b) is much better, (iii) why most pianists will pedal more frequently—e.g. as suggested under the music.

The opening of: Waltz in D♭ Op. 64, No. 1   **Chopin**

26

Pianists would have to be good at scales to play the above piece. Most music has at least bits and pieces of scales and broken chords in it.

Practising scales or some other exercise can be boring. So, some composers have written pieces consisting of just one type of difficulty. They are called STUDIES (ÉTUDES in French).

There are studies for scales, broken chords, arpeggios and other playing skills, and for every instrument.

The opening of: Study in C, Op. 10, No. 1   Chopin

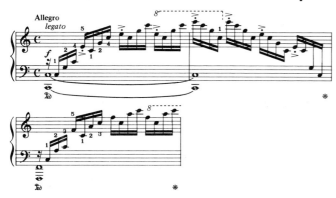

(e) Before listening to the above, discuss (i) what the pianist is practising in this study, (ii) the meaning of *8* and the small figures. Now as you listen, notice (iii) whether the RH has any rest from its practising, (iv) the hidden tune: which hand plays it? (v) the chords changing with each broken chord pattern.

Things to do

4. List all the letters played in the above extract (once each). What is the root of the chord used in each bar? Does this explain the pedal timing?

Major and perfect intervals

Only two chords are used in the first three bars of the Study, but many are used during the piece. Chord changes, whether the chords are 'solid' or 'broken', help make music interesting.

There are also different types of chords. These are best explained by first learning more about scales. Remember: there is the chromatic scale—a series of semitone steps (like a row of terraced houses):

there is the whole-tone scale—a series of tone steps (like a row of detached houses):

as well as the scale most people sing naturally, the major scale—a mixture of tones and semitones (with two pairs of 'semis'):

Things to do

5. Compare the above scales as they are played slowly, starting from the same pitch. Each time, follow the appropriate 'street diagram' with a finger. Listen for the difference between tones and semitones.

6. Listen to chromatic, whole-tone and major scales, each starting from several notes. Now identify each scale as an octave up or down them is played.

7. Now listen to phrases based on one or other of these scales. Identify the scale used.

8. Compare tones with semitones as each is played as two successive notes. Now try to tell which is played.

9. Similarly compare and then identify tones and semitones played simultaneously as a mixture. Which is the more clashing? Can they both be an interval of a 2nd?

The above street diagram shows that detached houses can be as much 'next door' as semis and terraced houses. In the major scale the closeness of 'next door' depends on where you live in the 'street'. So, the interval of a 2nd can be both a tone or a semitone.

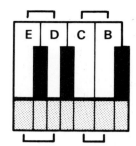

On the keys, the 2nds *seem* the same distance apart:

Inside the piano, they can be different:

There can also be more than one type of 3rd. On the keys, the 3rds *seem* equidistant:

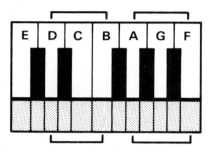

Inside the piano, they can be different:

There are different types of all intervals. However, there is a basic version of each one. From any note, the basic intervals are measured by going up a major scale. Every major scale must have the same intervals. The # and *b* of each key signature ensures that the T and ST pattern is always the same as C major. For example, here are these intervals from C, D, F, G and A:

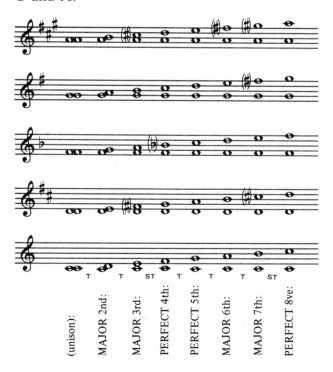

So, intervals do not just have numbers. They have a quality name as well.

Wider (or COMPOUND) intervals repeat these names through the next octaves. For example:

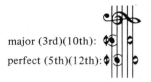

major (3rd)(10th):

perfect (5th)(12th):

As the same letters (and therefore sounds with a family likeness) are involved, 9ths are usually called 2nds, 10ths are called 3rds, and so on. Remember, the notes of any interval may be played

in succession, as part of a tune (melodic):

simultaneously, as part of a chord (harmonic): Intervals must always be measured upwards even when it means going backwards:

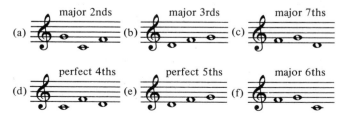

In your notebook

(i) (Copy, completing the words)
From any starting note, the intervals of ascending major scale are;—— 2nd, ——3rd, ——4th, ——5th, ——6th, ——7th and——octave.

Things to do

10. Name the major scale interval from the tonic up to the (a) dominant, (b) leading note, (c) mediant, (d) subdominant, (e) supertonic, (f) submediant.

11. Copy the following, adding the required interval above each note. Use # and *b* when necessary:

(a) major 2nds (b) major 3rds (c) major 7ths

(d) perfect 4ths (e) perfect 5ths (f) major 6ths

12. First compare the sounds of these interval mixtures: major 2nd (clashing), major 3rd (pleasant) and perfect 5th (bare). Now recognise the interval as a variety of them are played. Is a major 2nd a tone or semitone?

13. Now recognise the same intervals when played melodically up or down.

Have you wondered why the basic intervals don't all have the same quality name? There are several reasons why 8ves, 4ths and 5ths have special names. One is that these were the only interval mixtures allowed in much medieval church music. The 3rds that we find so pleasant were considered 'imperfect' and not suitable for use. Although musical fashions have now changed, the names have stuck.

(f) Return to earlier 'fashions'. Hear medieval music featuring perfect 4th/5th mixtures.

Any treble players join the descants/tenors in playing known scales with the same fingering. Next, play simple tunes by ear, also using the same fingering. Why does this sound medieval?

Treble players must now stop 'cheating' and learn to read music properly. On the treble recorder the F major scale is fingered the same as C on the descant:

At first, when reading music just remember the tonic and dominant 'landmarks' in key F: Then learn to move by step from a 'landmark':

Finally, treble and descant/tenor players play the F major scale together. Trebles will sound a B♭ without realising it.

In the next song, slur the notes where indicated. Music suitable for the treble (as well as descant/tenor) is marked Tr. This first part is 'landmarks', the second steps from these.

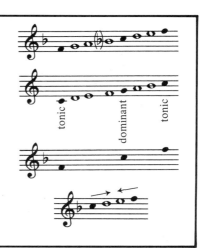

A song from Australia: 'Waltzing Matilda'

Things to do

14. Clap the above song, saying the rhythm words 'walk' |, 'running' ♫, 'scampering' ♫, 'long jumping' ♫ and 'supersonic' ♫.

15. Play/sing the song and parts. Is it a waltz? Why is a separate part harder than a score? Why does the first part sound like a bugle call? Notice the pleasant effect of a change of key and a new chord on beat 2 of bar 13.

Major chords

The major scale not only spells out the basic intervals.

Its   1st (tonic)   3rd (mediant)   5th degrees (dominant)

also spell out a MAJOR CHORD

A major chord therefore consists of

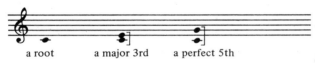

a root   a major 3rd   a perfect 5th

As the key signature ensures that every major scale has a major 3rd and a perfect 5th, each scale spells out its own major chord. You can see above how the C major scale produces the C major chord. Similarly, for example, the A major scale produces the A major chord:

Tonic triads (I) of major keys will always be major chords. So will dominant triads (V):

I   V   I

As the key C dominant triad
   is the same as the key G tonic triad,
   it must also be a major chord.

Although there are other types of chord, it is assumed that chords called just C, G, etc. are really C major, G major, etc.

30

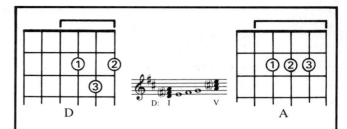

D   D: I   V   A

Guitarists were not expected to accompany 'Waltzing Matilda'. Some keys are particularly awkward for certain instruments. For example, guitarists do not like keys with flats.

Your new chords are I V in a sharp key. Practise (a) each separately, (b) changing between them.

Things to do

16. Listen to a 'handful' of Cs (roots) and Gs (5ths) played on the piano. Compare this bare medieval sound with the richness when just one E (3rd) is added to complete the C major triad.

17. Assemble instruments to play chords I and V in key D. Accompany previous two-chord songs (page 6) with DIY chords using any method/style (page 9).

18. Get into four groups. Each one assemble instruments to play just one of the following major chords. (Any guitarists need only finger one chord each.) Next, decide on playing style (ii) or (iii) (page 9). Now play your DIY chords in turn as indicated:

(a) |2/4 G | C | D | A | C | G | A | D ||

(b) |2/4 G | D | A | C | G | D | C | A ||

(c) |2/4 D | C | C | A | A | G | C | D ||

(d) |2/4 G | C | A | D | A | D | G | G ||

Later, play all four chord progressions in succession.

19. Repeat 18, using playing methods (b) or (c) (page 9) (any guitarists now changing chords).

20. Write/play a phrase to fit one of the progressions. Use only chord notes. No leger lines and jumps greater than a 3rd may be used. Accidentals can be used, as in this example:

(a)   G   C   D   A   C   G   A   D

7 MINOR ALTERATIONS

Minor intervals

Things to do

1. Repeat Chapter 6 (8, 9 and 12).

Tones and semitones are both 2nds.

We know the tone, e.g.

is a major 2nd. There-
fore, the semitone, e.g.
must be another kind of
2nd.

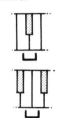

Every major 2nd, e.g.

can be squashed together
by a semitone, either by
lowering the upper note:
or by raising the lower
one:

All major intervals can be similarly treated:
any major

squashed by a semitone becomes a MINOR

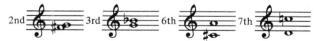

'Minor' does not mean less important than
'major'. Also, making an interval minor does
not affect its basic mixture flavour. Both major
and minor 2nds have the clashing 'next door'
sound. Both major and minor 3rds are pleasant.

When writing or working
out an interval above any
note, use a major scale
'ruler':

For example to write a
minor 3rd above A:
First find the
major 3rd by going
up the major scale:
Then squash it down
by a semitone:
To measure this 7th:
First see if it is
a major 7th by going
up the major scale:
As it has been squashed
by a semitone, it is therefore a minor 7th.

Remember, when modifying a basic interval,
do not change letter names. Further, notice (a)
flattening naturals has the same effect as (b)
naturalising sharps, (c) sharpening naturals has
the same effect as (d) naturalising flats:

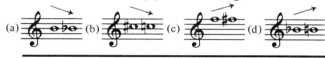

Things to do

2. Change the intervals of Chapter 6, 11(a),
(b), (c) and (f) to minor 2nds, 3rds, 7ths and
6ths (i) by lowering upper notes, (ii) by raising
lower notes.

3. Copy the following, writing the required interval above each note. Use the major 'ruler':

4. Identify these intervals:

5. Hear and identify these melodic intervals.
Why must you always measure upwards?

6. Sing (a) a major 2nd (b) a major 3rd above given notes. Work them out by going up major scales in your head. Now sing minor 2nds and 3rds. First work out the major interval and then squash it back a semitone.

7. In groups of five players with conductor, take/share instruments to play these intervals. Perform and record/play back if possible:

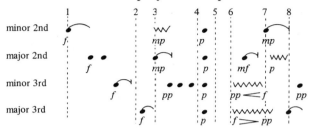

8. Hear two pupils play this slowly using two beaters, damping in rests. Notice the clashes between major and minor 3rds/chords:

9. Compare the sound of major and minor 3rds played harmonically. Now identify them.

Minor chords

Although both kinds of 3rd make a pleasant mixture, minor 3rds usually sound more 'sad'.
Major 3rds usually sound more 'happy':

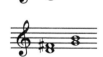

This is also true for 3rds when part of a tune. In Chopin's Funeral March, changing to a major 3rd at X makes it happy!

(transposed)   X

etc.

Descant/tenor players practise these broken chords (up and down) in the following rhythms:

Treble players similarly practise the F major chord. There is a part based on these triad 'landmarks' in the next song.

Things to do

10. The above is the slow movement of a piano sonata. Listen to the extract (and more, if possible). Compare the effect of the major 3rd variation. Play both versions.

It is the major 3rd (and the perfect 5th) that makes a major chord 'happy'. Making the 3rd minor: (but keeping the 5th): produces a MINOR TRIAD (CHORD):

Remember, the 1st, 3rd and 5th degrees of every major scale spell out a major triad, e.g.:

Triads of Dmaj (min)   Gmaj (min)   Amaj (min)

Each one, with its major 3rd made minor, becomes a (bracketed minor) triad (chord).

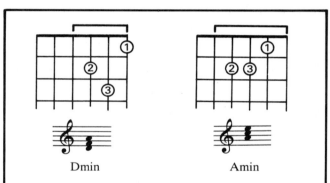

Dmin   Amin

When you can play these minor chords, practise changing between them (four strums each).
Next, compare the sound as you change from A minor to A major, D minor to D major.

In your notebook

(i) (Copy, completing the words)
Major intervals squashed by a——become ——. Major triads consist of a root, a——3rd and a ——5th. Lowering the 3rd by a semitone creates a ——triad. ——3rds and—— chords tend to sound sad.

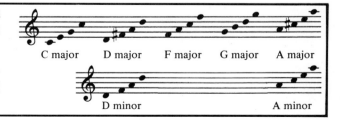

C major   D major   F major   G major   A major

D minor   A minor

Things to do

11. Write out these triads on the treble stave: C major, D major, F major, G major, A major.

12. Rewrite 11 as minor triads.

13. Assemble instruments to play the triads of 11 and 12, as DIY chords. Play each major chord in turn, followed by its minor version, accompanied by the same chord on the piano.

14. Now identify chords played on the piano as major or minor. Compare (a) simple three-note triads on the same root, (b) as (a) but on different roots, (c) fully spread-out chords.

15. Each take or share a fading-sound instrument to play A, C, C# or E at any octave. All play simultaneously and listen to the clashing effect as A major and minor chords sound together. Repeat, damping (a) the Cs, (b) the C#s at a signal. Name the chord produced each time.

16. Get into groups of five and practise the following.

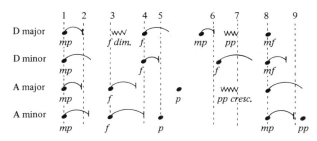

Each pupil play the three-note triad on a fading-sound instrument using three beaters (any guitarists strumming one of the chords, damping with the LH if necessary):

17. Prepare to play DIY chords for the following song. Practise them as the song is played on the piano. Do the mainly minor chords make it sound sad?

(a) Listen to different performances of the following song. Are the rhythms or words different? If the key is the same and your instruments are in tune with the recording, play with it:

A folk song from England: 'Scarborough Fair'

Minor scales

Not everything about a major scale is major (or perfect). Only from the tonic are all the intervals major (or perfect), e.g. F major:

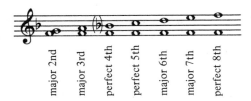

major 2nd · major 3rd · perfect 4th · perfect 5th · major 6th · major 7th · perfect 8th

The intervals between other degrees of the scale can have a different quality, e.g.:

measuring from the mediant to the dominant gives a minor 3rd:

This means that any major chord—for example, the tonic triad (I) of key F major—not only has:

a major 3rd from the root: but a minor 3rd above it.

Lowering the 3rd a semitone for minor chords reverses the two intervals. Any minor chord, for example, D minor has:

a minor 3rd from the root: but a major 3rd above it.

Either way round, in both major and minor chords, the 5th remains perfect:

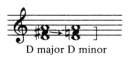
D major   D minor

The lower (major) 3rd of a major triad is the *upper* 3rd of a minor triad:

F major   D minor

Pairs of chords like this are related to each other in a special way. They are the tonic chords of major and MINOR SCALES that share the same key signature—and same basic 'track':

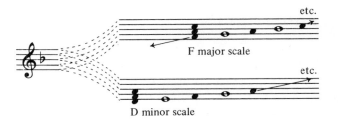
F major scale
etc.

D minor scale
etc.

These two scales (keys) are the RELATIVE MAJOR and RELATIVE MINOR of each other. The relative minor of F major is a scale starting two degrees down the F major scale:

Every major scale:

has a relative minor scale:

using the same basic stairway:

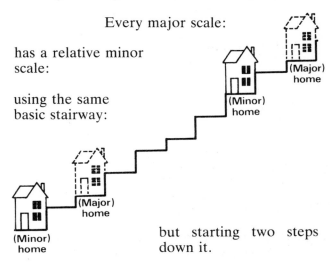

(Major) home

(Minor) home

(Major) home

(Minor) home

but starting two steps down it.

The notes are basically the same—the changed T and ST pattern creating the 'sad' minor flavour. After all, seven words when in a different order would have a changed meaning!

It is the opening minor 3rd that makes minor key tunes sad—and their tonic chord minor:

Here are another pair of related major and minor scales. These share the (open) key signature. The minor scale degree names are the same, but start from the new tonic:

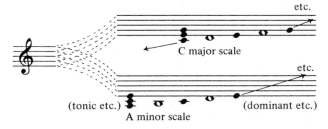
C major scale
etc.

(tonic etc.)   (dominant etc.)
A minor scale
etc.

Always assume scales, keys and chords are major, unless minor is indicated (abbrev. A min, Am or by use of small letter: a).

34

Things to do

18. Seven pupils stand in a row with C major-scale chime bars C D E F G A B. (a) Play in turn up the scale. What is the effect of ending on B? (b) Move A and B to the lower end and play the A minor scale. Why does the wrong octave make little difference? What does this tell you about the key signatures of C major and A minor?

19. Sing the first five notes of a major scale to la (or solfa). Now, sing just the third and fifth degrees. Next, count the third degree as a new tonic and sing to the third degree of that major scale. Discuss what happens.

20. Listen to and then sing the first five notes of the F major scale up and down accompanied by an F major chord. Similarly, match D major and D minor scales with their respective chords. Now try singing a D major five-note scale against a D minor chord—and vice versa. Which degree causes you trouble?

21. Play this major key phrase. Then compare it in its minor key version. D major and D minor do *not* share the same key signature! Now compare/play themes A and F (page 38).

D major   D minor

22. Rewrite the funeral march on page 32 in key D major, changing the key signature. Play both versions.

23. First play this phrase as written. Then rewrite and play in its A minor version. Which do you prefer?

24. Compose or improvise (later writing it down) your own two-phrase melody in key D or A major. Begin and end on the tonic note and use only the first five degrees of the scale. Use your own time and rhythm, that of 23. Rewrite in its minor key version. Practise both versions and play to the class, voting for the best.

25. A four-bar phrase will be played in key D or A major/minor, beginning and ending on the tonic in (a) the rhythm of 21, (b) any 2/4 rhythm. Write it down on the treble stave, using the correct key signature.

26. Work out the relative minor keys of G and D major. Write the tonic triads of these keys on the treble stave, with key signatures.

27. On the treble stave, without signatures, write the following as semibreves:
Key D minor: subdominant, dominant, mediant;
Key E minor: tonic, supertonic, dominant;
Key B minor: supertonic, tonic, dominant.

28. Turn to page 25. Compare bars 1–2 and 1–4 respectively of each extract played in A minor and D minor. Compare key signatures also.

29. Identify short phrases as being in a major or minor key (a) harmonised, (b) unaccompanied.

In your notebook

(ii) (Copy, completing the words)
Every major scale has a related——scale starting two——lower. For example, the——minors of C, F and G major are A,—and—minor.

The following tone poem describes the River Vltava (Moldau). Its nationalistic features include Czech dance rhythms such as the polka. Extract A, in E minor, is like a minor version of 'Twinkle, twinkle, little star'. Extract B is in the relative major key of G:

Two themes from 'Vltava'   Smetana

(b) Hear the first four scenes from 'Vltava'.
(i) The Source: A flute, soon joined by a second in imitation, represent two springs. Pizz. strings (drips) then enter. Immediately after two triangle taps, the cellos take over the flute tune.
(ii) The River: Follow its flowing theme (A).
   Which instrument(s) plays it? Notice the cello tune still underneath.
(iii) Forest Hunting Scene: Identify the chief instrument(s).
   Why are they appropriate? Repeated notes lead to:
(iv) Village Wedding: Follow Theme (B). Which instruments play this polka?

35

8 MINOR ROAD WORKS

Harmonic minor scale

Not all two-chord songs are in a major key. Here is one in D minor:

A folk song: **'Go Tell Aunt Mary'**

Melodic/Class Instruments [incl. 3rd, 5th jumps]

1. Go tell Aunt Ma - ry, go tell Aunt Ma - ry, go tell Aunt Ma - ry, her poor old cow is dead.

Things to do

1. Sing or play this tune with a D minor chord accompaniment throughout. Which bars require the dominant chord?
2. What key signature is required to change the above tune into D major? Which note is changed? Repeat 1 in D major and D minor.

The above tune uses just the first five notes of the scale:

In D major, the new key signature changes only one of these notes:

Notice how the tonic and dominant chords match their keys:

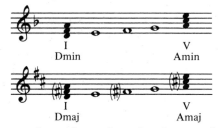

Unfortunately, when the dominant chord is minor, it does not have the 'going home' effect.

Things to do

3. Assemble instruments to play DIY chords I and V in keys D major/minor as above. Repeat 1 and 2, working out where to use chord V. Compare the effect of V in each version.

In any major key, the (major) seventh note of the scale is attracted to the tonic, just a semitone above—hence its name of leading note. As it contains the leading note, chord V is also attracted to chord I:

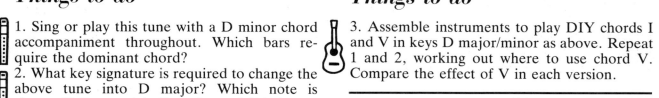

There is no corresponding attraction in the basic minor scale—the final step is a tone:

This not only makes chord V minor, the minor 7th in the scale also makes tunes sound medieval (modal) or 'folky'. Minor scales are therefore usually modernised by raising their seventh degree a semitone, using an accidental:

This not only makes chord V major, it creates the magnetic semitone that draws chord V to chord I.

This form of minor scale, in which the seventh note is sharpened, is the one normally used for chord-building. It is therefore called the HARMONIC MINOR SCALE.

Every basic minor scale can be changed in this way. For example, here is A harmonic minor:

Although other modifications are possible, none of the changes affect the first five notes. Remember, these spell out the minor tonic chord and establish the general 'minor flavour'. References just to a minor scale will now always mean the harmonic version.

'Scarborough Fair' (page 33) is a modal tune. It uses the 'white' note D scale. Much of 'Greensleeves' is based on a similar scale. The bracketed accidental shows how uncertain we are when interpreting old music notation:

In your notebook

(i) (Copy, completing the words)
The——minor scale is the one used for chord-building. To write any one of these, (a) first lay the basic minor track, using the——major key signature, (b) then raise its——degree a semitone by using an——sharp or natural.

Things to do

4. Sing these ascending scales with the piano, each time stopping at the seventh degree: (a) D major. Do you feel the 'magnetic' pull between the leading note and the tonic? (b) The basic D minor scale. This time there should be less of a pull upwards at the end. (c) D harmonic minor. Again, you should find it difficult to stop at the leading note.
5. First sing 'Scarborough Fair' (page 33) as written. Notice the old-fashioned modal fla-

vour—especially the effect of the minor 7th (C). Now hear the last phrase (a) modernised with a C#, (b) in D major with both an F# and C#. Sing this phrase in all three versions and discuss which you prefer.
6. Sing the above opening of 'Greensleeves' (a) as written without the B♭, (b) with B♭, (c) in D minor, with a C# (d) in D major with F# and C#. After discussing which you prefer suggest why the details of old music are often uncertain. Finally, identify the versions (a-d) as they are played in a different order.
7. Repeat 3, this time using the proper dominant chord for the D minor version.
8. Write out one octave ascending of the scales of E minor and B minor in semibreves. Use the key signature of the relative major key and modify the seventh degrees.
9. Write the tonic chords of E min and B min, this time without key signatures. Write as simple three-note triads on the treble stave. Now rewrite as the chords of E major and B major by raising their thirds a semitone.
10. In groups, prepare to play the following DIY chords:

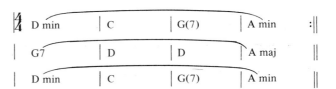

After suitable practice, each group play to the class. What is the form of this music? Now, also in groups, experiment to produce another four-phrase chord progression. Use 3/4 or 4/4 time and all (or some) of the chords in any order, repeating the same one in succession if you like. When each is played to the class, vote (a) for the most interesting progression, (b) for the best performance. If you like, later write a tune to fit the winner of (a). Use any rhythm, begin and end on any note, but otherwise follow the suggestions given in Chapter 3, 6. Is it likely that your tune (and chords) will have a normal major or minor key flavour? Finally, perform the tunes with DIY chord accompaniment.
11. First write out 'Go tell Aunt Mary' (page 36), adding I or V under the first bar and at every chord change. Now write out the tune transposed upwards into key A minor. Think about the new key signature required and the pitch of the first note. Add I and V as before.

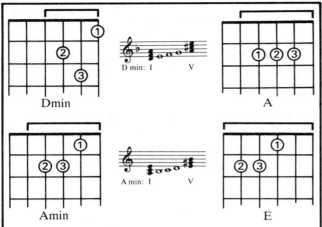

Dmin

D min: I   V

Amin

A min: I   V

A

E

Guitarists only need the chord of E major to be able to play I and V in keys D minor and A minor. For reference, the other chords are shown again.

Things to do

12. Assemble instruments to play DIY chords I and V in keys D minor and A minor. Now perform 'Go tell Aunt Mary' in both these keys. Sing and/or play the tune with DIY chord accompaniment.

13. Try singing minor key versions of some of the two-chord songs on page 6. Choose either D or A minor, to suit your singing compass. After listening to the first five notes of the minor scale you should not find this difficult. At first just sing with piano accompaniment. Later, sing and/or play the tune by ear with DIY chord accompaniment as in 12.

Romantic piano concertos

Minor keys were very popular in the nineteenth century. So were concertos. Many people first come to enjoy 'classical' music through one of the great concertos of this period.

Schumann wrote four symphonies, but only this one piano concerto. However, it has become one of the most popular pieces in the REPERTOIRE of concert pianists. Its main theme begins by spelling out the sad minor 3rd of the key:

Piano concerto in A Minor, Op. 54: Opening theme of First Movement   Schumann

Later varied forms of this theme:

38

(a) First hear Theme A played on the piano. Notice the sad opening minor 3rd. Next, hear each varied form, discussing how each is similar/different from A. Schumann never changes the opening descending four-note shape.

Although other themes appear in the first-movement, concentrate on the above. Now, in this sonata form movement, listen for:
(i) Dramatic piano flourish followed by A, first in the woodwind and then on solo piano. This is followed by piano RH broken chords with a tune in the LH and/or strings.
(ii) After two loud ascending and descending piano 8ve scales separated by a tutti, a mainly descending piano chordal theme leads to
(iii) B (= A in the relative major key of C);
(iv) C on the clarinet. Notice the big jump upwards. This is repeated. The piano descending broken chord accompaniment continues with the top note of each group accented to create a melody. Wait for an oboe inversion of the opening, followed by the clarinet as before.
(v) The piano RH takes up a new theme from the oboe, followed by this theme in the LH with RH broken chords. A tutti leads to
(vi) D, with new key and time signatures. A clarinet repeat is followed by 'conversation', alternating the piano and clarinet/flute in various keys. This is interrupted by
(vii) a piano flourish similar to the beginning, alternating several times with the strings. A long piano 8ve passage leads to
(viii) E on the piano, continuing higher in a sequence. Which instrument doubles the piano tune? This is followed by rather similar alternating phrases on the piano and wind. The piano eventually descends in a long diminuendo and ritardando over a bass pedal E, ending on the chord of E major. As the dominant of A minor, this leads home to the tonic key:
(ix) as (i) but without opening piano flourish

(ii) follows as before. Notice the surprise *ff* chord after the first piano 8ve scale. This time, the descending chordal theme leads to
(x) F (= A in key A major). Again this is immediately followed by (iv) and (v) this time also mostly in A major. This leads to
(xi) the solo cadenza, fully written out by the composer. Notice the modulations, an exciting quick chord passage and a return to the opening theme in A minor in the LH under long shakes in the RH. Soon, during another long shake, the orchestra returns with the coda:
(xii) G, in the wind, accompanied by piano broken chords. Notice a changed time/tempo and syncopation. Very soon the first four-note rhythm is used in quick alternation between instruments. Finally, with a crescendo, the opening of A appears for the last time (oboe). An A minor piano arpeggio and four tutti chords conclude the movement.

Compared with classical concertos what is unusual about the start of this movement? Now discuss the meaning of: repertoire, melodic inversion, tutti, shake, cadenza, coda.

(b) Compare the 1st movement of Grieg's only piano concerto with that of the Schumann, written about twenty years earlier in 1845. Deeply nationalistic, many of Grieg's themes have the flavour of Norwegian folk music. Many of them also begin (or include) tonic, leading note, dominant (or similar descending shape). First make yourself familiar with the sound of this in major/minor keys by hearing particularly the bracketed parts of themes A–F. x and ⌐⎯⎯⎯ indicate variations/inversions of this pattern.

After a drum roll and piano flourish (A) the first important theme includes B. Continue, identifying extracts as they first occur/are repeated.

Piano Concerto in A minor, Op 16: Some First Movement themes   **Grieg**

Virtuoso composers

The Schumann and Grieg concertos are certainly not easy to play. Some nineteenth-century virtuoso players, however, deliberately wrote difficult music—to show off their playing technique. When the Italian violinist Paganini played works like the following in London, his fans tried to touch him to see if he was real! Titles like CAPRICE and RHAPSODY do not mean anything in particular:

Caprice (and Variations):   **Paganini**

(c) Hear the above work. In the Variations detect traces of the theme as the piano simultaneously plays either it or the underlying chords. Why is the work difficult?

Many composers, fascinated by Paganini's minor key theme, have since written sets of variations on it. Do not expect most variations to sound like new tunes—as in the Schumann. Any variation usually 'flogs' just one or two musical devices. These include:
(i) Dividing each note up into faster ones using (SC) scales, (BC) broken chords, (AP) arpeggios, (SH) shakes, etc.
(ii) Changing (H) harmony, (S) speed, (T) time, (R) rhythm, (K) key—including minor to major.
(iii) Featuring (J) jumps, (O) octaves, (SY) syncopation, (ST) staccato, (D) dynamics, (B) theme in bass.
The Brahms set of variations is one of the most difficult of all piano works. The Rachmaninov set can be counted as 'Romantic' in style—even though the composer died as recently as 1943.

Born in Russia, he later lived in America. One of the world's greatest pianists, Rachmaninov's own recording of the Rhapsody may be available. The work contains a famous example of melodic inversion. The direction of each interval of the theme is inverted—just like this:

(d) Hear Brahm's 'Variations on a Theme of Paganini'. Write one or more of the letters given earlier to match each variation.
(e) Compare Rachmaninov's Rhapsody on this Theme. Detect theme snippets, or treat as (d). Finger a 'mirror reflection' on the Theme during the slow 'Romantic' upside-down variation.

Things to do

14. Play a slow ascending scale of A minor (harmonic). Notice the awkward interval between the sixth and seventh degrees. Try to sing the scale to 'la' unaccompanied! Repeat both playing and singing, raising the sixth degree to F#. This modification to the minor scale is often made for the sake of the melody.

15. Look at the A minor Paganini Theme above. Compare the effect as the first four bars are played slowly on the piano (a) as written, (b) with the F natural of the harmonic minor scale. Try to plays bars 1–4 on a xylophone/recorder.

16. Still referring to the Theme, find (a) one-bar and two-bar sequences, (b) modulations to D minor and C major.

Assignment

(A) List famous present-day virtuosi on the piano, violin etc., adding their nationality and any pictures. Use the *Radio Times*, newspapers, record magazines, programmes.

9 TIME FOR A CHANGE

Different beat notes

The nineteenth century was not that 'Romantic' for most people. While the wealthy could afford to go to hear beautiful piano concertos, the poor often found it difficult to make ends meet. In Britain, the workhouses set up by the Poor Law Amendment Act of 1843 were filled with debtors and other unfortunates. In these, conditions were made deliberately harsh, and husbands were separated from wives to prevent more paupers being born. Workhouse children were frequently apprenticed as chimney sweeps, factory hands and even sailors. From the age of seven their masters owned them until they were twenty-one. Many nineteenth-century folk songs paint an unhappy picture of life during the Industrial Revolution. Here is a good example:

'The Captain's Apprentice'

Melodic/Class Instruments [incl. 3rd, 4th, 5th jumps]

Em   D   Em   Am   Em

1. A boy to me was bound ap-pren-tice Be-cause his pa-rents they were so poor; I

G   Em   D   Em

took him from St. Jame-s's work-house, All for to sail on some Spa-nish shore.

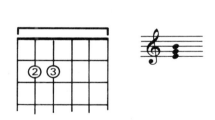

One new chord is needed to play the above song. It is the easiest of all. Practise it in alternation with the other chords required.

This song sounds 'folky' because it uses the basic E minor scale with no sharpened 7th degree. It is also written with a minim beat. If minim 'shoes' replace crotchet ones:

$\frac{2}{4}$ The upper figure is unchanged as the number of beats is the same: the lower figure changes to show the value of the new beat unit: $\frac{2}{2}$

Things to do

1. Assemble instruments to play (a) DIY chords for the song, (b) its melody. Accompany it played/sung. Now discuss (i) whether the song uses the E harmonic minor scale, (ii) its time signature/rhythm.

41

Just as distances can be measured in feet, metres etc., so the same music can be 'measured' in different units. The signature's lower figure gives the American name of the beat unit used. As suggested before, on page 16,

It is often   4 (quarter note beats)

but it can be 2 (half note beats)

or 8 (eighth note beats)

New shoes do not affect normal walking speed. Neither need new musical 'shoes' affect music tempi. Other things change though.

With the familiar crotchet beat 'shoes',

quavers are half-beat notes
minims are two beats

With minim beat 'shoes',

crotchets are half-beat notes
semibreves are two beats

Notice how the different note values adapt to the same counting system. It does mean, however, that it is not always correct to say that a crotchet is a one-beat note! Although counting can always be used to help you perform in the right rhythm, it might be confusing to adapt word rhythms to other beat units:

['walk   walk   run - ning   run - ning']

Interesting syncopation occurs in bar 2 (3 and 6) of 'The Captain's Apprentice' where a long note starts between beats:

Things to do

2. First discuss why 4 = crotchet and 2 = minim. What would the lower figure of the time signature be if the beat unit was a quaver? Now write out the above 'Land of Hope and Glory' rhythm using a quaver beat. Include the appropriate time signature and add beat numbers as before.

3. Clap this rhythm while looking at the 4/4 beat version (a) saying the rhythm words 'walk', 'running' and 'crawl', (b) counting the beat numbers. Repeat (b) looking at the 4/2 version and then at your 4/8 beat one. Make all performances the same speed, setting your body 'clock' to run at minim or quaver 'ticks' instead of crotchet ones. Now three groups clap the different versions simultaneously at the same tempo.

4. Repeat 3 at other tempi. Make minim/quaver beats go both faster and slower than crotchets.

5. Rewrite the following using (a) minim beats, (b) quaver beats. Repeat 3 and 4, with this rhythm. What rhythm word can be used for ♩. ♪ ?

'Jin-gle bells,   jin - gle bells,   jin-gle all   the   way.'

Finally, discuss (a) when a crotchet is not a one-beat note, (b) whether crotchets last for 1 second, (c) if a minim is ever shorter than a crotchet, (d) when a minim must be twice as long as a crotchet, (e) whether minim beats encourage slower tempi, (f) whether a dot adds a crotchet/one more beat to a note?

'Changing shoes' is just a change in the way music is written (notation). It does not necessarily change the musical effect. For example, the following are identical rhythms which could all be performed at the same tempo:

(a) 'One man went to mow, | went to mow a | mea-dow.'

(b)

(c)

This also reminds you that the value of any dot is determined by the value of the note dotted. 'Sausages on sticks' show this even more clearly:

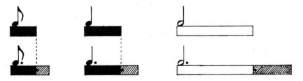

So, if your wages were 'dotted', it would be like having a 50 per cent rise!

42

Simple and compound time

When the beat is an (undotted) quaver, crotchet or minim, the time is said to be SIMPLE (meaning straightforward—not easy!).

$\frac{2}{8}$ $\frac{2}{4}$ or $\frac{2}{2}$($\mathbb{C}$)   are all SIMPLE DUPLE TIME

$\frac{3}{8}$ $\frac{3}{4}$ or $\frac{3}{2}$ are all SIMPLE TRIPLE TIME

$\frac{4}{8}$ $\frac{4}{4}$($\mathbb{C}$) or $\frac{4}{2}$ are all SIMPLE QUADRUPLE TIME

When beats are dotted, the time is said to be COMPOUND. Again, the dotted crotchet is not always the note value used as the beat. The following, therefore, are also identical rhythms:

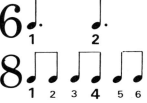

$\frac{6}{16}$ $\frac{6}{8}$ or $\frac{6}{4}$ are COMPOUND DUPLE TIME

$\frac{9}{16}$ $\frac{9}{9}$ or $\frac{9}{4}$ are COMPOUND TRIPLE TIME

$\frac{12}{16}$ $\frac{12}{8}$ or $\frac{12}{4}$ are COMPOUND QUADRUPLE TIME

Remember, compound time signatures do not give the number of beats in a bar. If they did, $\frac{2}{\text{♩}}$ would be $\frac{2}{3/8}$ over (dotted crotchet = ¼ + ⅛)

Instead, the upper figure gives the number of thirds of a beat, e.g.:
The lower figure represents the American name of each third of a beat:

In slow tempi (or when practising) thirds could be counted instead of beats. Alternatively, rhythm words could be used (e.g. 'walk', 'galloping', 'skipping'). In both simple and compound times, any hooks 'hold hands' within the same beat.

Unusual times are possible. Subdivide bars into twos and threes:

Things to do

6. Clap/count rhythms (a–c) at one tempo, looking at each in turn. Repeat at different tempi as in 4. Similarly treat rhythms (d–f).
7. Clap rhythm (e). Start slowly, counting the thirds. Repeat at gradually faster tempi until it is easier and more musical to count with the main beats. Clap again at this tempo, saying the rhythm words. Finally, discuss why compound time signatures do not show the beats.
8. Rewrite the first phrase of 'Scarborough Fair' (page 33) in both 9/16 and 9/4 time.
9. Write the time signatures of the following bars (the notes shown are beat notes):

10. Give the time signatures of the following:
   (a) two crotchets in a bar;
   (b) four minims in a bar;
   (c) three dotted minims in a bar;
   (d) four half notes in a bar;
   (e) two dotted eighth notes in a bar;
   (f) simple quadruple time (quaver beats);
   (g) compound triple time (dotted quaver beats).
11. List compound time songs/music in this and other music/song books.
12. Identify as simple or compound time:
   'For he's a Jolly Good Fellow',
   'My old man's a dustman', 'Happy birthday to you',
   'I've got a lovely bunch of coconuts',
   'It's a long way to Tipperary', 'Jingle bells',
   Now work out the time signature of each using a (dotted) crotchet beat.

In your notebook

(i) (Copy, filling in the gaps)
In simple——the beat unit may be a quaver, crotchet or——. The beat unit is a dotted note in——time. The upper figure of simple time gives the number of—— in the bar, while the lower figure represents the——name of the beat unit. In——time, the figures represent the number and value of thirds of a beat.

Over the centuries music notation has gradually changed. In the Renaissance, it looked generally more 'white:

From then on, shorter and shorter values were used as the beat note. Since the eighteenth century, the crotchet (and dotted crotchet) has been the beat unit most commonly used. This is why the crotchet is often called (incorrectly?) a one-beat note. However, the beat unit chosen by the composer or printer is really just a matter of taste—or appearance. Some hymn books have minim beats. Longer notes look more dignified! In the following, a quaver beat is used in the Scherzo. Quaver beats need not always be fast, though! Mendelssohn wrote the overture when he was only seventeen! The Scherzo and other Incidental Music—originally intended as interludes (ENTRACTES) or background for Shakespeare's play—were composed seventeen years later (see opus numbers):

Midsummer Night's Dream Mendelssohn
Themes from Overture, Op. 21

Themes from Scherzo Op. 61, No. 1

(a) Discuss the play's outline before hearing the overture. It is Programme Music, as Mendelssohn wants you to get in the right mood or think about characters/events. Notice:
(i) Soft opening rising wind chords (Fairyland/night). Minor keys are not always sad!

(ii) A fast staccato upper strings passage (fairies) interrupted twice by a mysterious wind chord (magic spells);
(iii) Theme A tutti (day festivities) followed by B, backed by horns (hunting party);
(iv) Two *ff* descending woodwind scales separated by a short string fanfare. A long tutti ends suddenly and softly in the wind;
(v) Theme C (Hermia and Helena) immediately followed by D, a similar, descending theme on violins and then flute. This is interrupted by
(vi) a short/wind brass fanfare (horns of Elfland), repeated after a legato string theme. The strings continue until
(vii) a repeating *ff* bass note ushers in Theme E (Bottom's ass's head). Notice the bracketed 'hee haws'. This is repeated and continued. Continue, recognising and following the above themes as they recur. Listen also for prominent horn notes and violin pizzicato.

Fairy music similar to (ii) returns three more times. The last time it ends with a pause on the mysterious wind chord. After further wind chords, recognise which of the above themes returns very slowly in the violins. The movement ends as it began, with rising wind chords.
(b) Hear the Scherzo. Mendelssohn is noted for this kind of fast, light, magical music. If you could see a score, you would notice that almost every bar is filled with dancing semiquavers.
(i) Theme F begins the movement, and instruments pass this and similar themes around in imitation and 'whispered' musical 'conversation'.
(ii) Theme G enters *pp* and staccato, with quaver woodwind chords. An immediate repeat is extended by a rising sequence. G returns three more times, try to guess when. Do not be fooled by the crescendos! After the last time, the flautist has to play two hundred and forty continuous semiquavers! (Does he breathe?) The movement then ends with Theme F on the clarinets.

Discuss how Mendelssohn uses tunes, chords, instruments, dynamics and tempi in his 'word painting'.
(c) Listen to the Wedding March from this work. After the rising tonic chord build-up on the trumpets, the first theme (X) begins with a memorable chord. Theme Y follows. List the reappearances of X and Y as you listen.
(d) Hear the second movement of Tchaikovsky's 6th Symphony. Count the 5/4 time, working out how it is best counted:

$$1 \quad 2 \quad 3 \quad 1 \quad 2 \quad \text{or} \quad 1 \quad 2 \quad 1 \quad 2 \quad 3$$

10 HOLDING HANDS

Note and rest grouping

Things to do

1. Refer to Themes A (page 44) and E (page 39). Discuss the meaning of $\mathbf{\mathrm{C}\!\!\!|}$ and $\mathbf{C}$. Now rewrite these themes in 2/4 and 4/2 time respectively.
2. Rewrite Theme F (page 44) in 3/4.

Note values with hooks should 'hold hands' within each beat or part of a beat, as in these original versions:

This makes each beat's-worth clear. We need this reminder, as the time signature (unlike the key) only appears at the beginning of the first line. In compound time, the same rule applies. For example, from pages 37 and 38:

However, printers do not always group thus.

There are also proper exceptions to just one beats-worth holding hands, e.g.

A complete bar of quavers in these times:

A bar of semiquavers in this time

Four quavers in the first or second half of quadruple time:

In vocal music, some printers join notes that are sung to the same syllable.

Things to do

3. Check your note grouping in 1 and 2, and rewrite the following, grouping correctly:

(a)

(b)

(c)

(d)

4. Add beat numbers and clap, looking at (i) corrected versions, (ii) the above. Which is easier?
5. Rewrite 3 in 4/2, 3/4, 6/4 and 3/4 time. Add beats/clap at different tempi.
6. Rewrite, using dotted notes instead of ties:

(a)

(b)

7. Write down four-bar rhythms played one or more times. Begin with a four-bar framework and a given (dotted) crotchet beat time. Use 'shorthand' notation as in 6 for rhythms with notes of one beat plus (i) half/third beats, (ii) multiple beats, (iii) all known rhythms.
8. Repeat 7, but with other beat note values.
9. Rewrite 3(a) (correctly grouped), replacing the first note in bars 1, 2 and 4 with the appropriate rest. Clap and count the new rhythm.
10. Echo these rhythms.

(a)

(b)

(c)

(d)

Rests are grouped to make the beats clear. A separate rest is usually used for each beat:

Half note (𝅗𝅥) or minim rest: ▬

Quarter note (𝅘𝅥) or crotchet rest: 𝄽 ℽ

Eighth note (𝅘𝅥𝅮) or QUAVER REST; ℽ

Sixteenth note (𝅘𝅥𝅯) or SEMIQUAVER REST ℽ

The shorter rests may also be used for part of a beat. Often, more than one rest is used especially to make beat subdivision clearer.

As with notes, there are exceptions to the beat's-worth rule. In all times a whole note (o) or semibreve rest is used for a whole bar's rest. e.g.

A single rest is used for the first or second half of quadruple times:

Rests may also be dotted. Often, however, rests are added rather than dotted:

In the polonaise on page 25 the same rhythmic effect is created

by a rest   by a dot

To avoid confusing with 𝄽 , ℽ is rarely used. However, **c**rotchet **q**uaver should help you.

Things to do

11. Write the page 41 song in 3/4. Group correctly. Follow, clapping beats. Note syncopation.

12. Copy, adding a suitable rest(s) at x:

(a) |4/4 ... x ...| (b)|6/8 ... x ...| (c)|3/2 ... x ...|

(d)|3/8 x ... | (e)|4/4 ... x ...| (f)|12/8 x ... |

13. Practise/perform as in Chapter 4 (9):

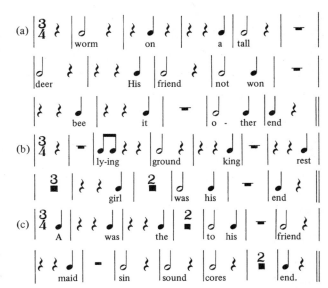

(a) worm on a tall
deer His friend not won
bee it o - ther end

(b) ly-ing ground king rest
girl was his end

(c) A was the to his friend
maid sin sound cores end.

Now, combine them and solve the mystery verse, recording the performance if possible.
14. Solve the word puzzle at (a)–(d) below by saying the lines (i) with both note and rest alternatives, (ii) ignoring those small notes/rests. Compare the effects. Rewrite correctly spelt.

Setting words to music

Stage One

(a) Make up a verse and write it down, separating the syllables.
(b) Read it through, accenting appropriate syllables. (c) Add accents and then bar lines. (d) Misspell syllables.

Stage Two

After choosing a suitable time signature, write one-beat notes when the beats and syllables match: write shorter notes for extra syllables: Write longer notes when there are spare beats:

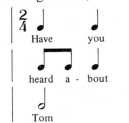

Have you
heard a - bout
Tom

(a) Have you herd a bough Tom (He)
(b) He thaw teas chair low was a vie -oh-lean
(c) Pooled the spy cow tan dent ride too,
(d) whole dit un - dare ease chin

Notice (i) how the extra bars satisfy the need for a four-bar phrase, (ii) even the final blank bar seems part of the rhythm, (iii) extending the last note or adding a rest are equally satisfactory, (iv) in (b) the weak (up) beat start (anacrusis) is also placed at the end of the previous phrase, (v) in 13(c) the opening anacrusis is subtracted from the final bar.

Provided accented syllables occur on beat one, (vi) words can be adapted to any time, (vii) alternative accent systems are often possible.

Things to do

15. Distribute the above verse between two or more parts as in 13. Avoid single quavers. Perform/record selected examples.

16. Re-set the above verse in 3/4 time. Some accents and spellings could be changed. Use only rhythms you know. Compare with 15.

17. Similarly, make up and set your own verse in any time. All perform and solve each mystery. Vote for the best.

18. Now fit the given rhythms to a tune. Use the following key G I-V plan and add key signature, words and slurs. Choose only chord notes (and ones you can play). Begin and end as you like, but include no intervals greater than a 5th.

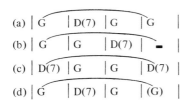

19. Modify these tunes in one or two places by

(a) substituting  for

(b) replacing a single note with two slurred chord notes. A varied rhythm can be seen at Z in the Schubert song on page 48. Award marks as your songs are played. All sing/play the winning song. Add DIY chord accompaniment.

20. Sing/play the next song. Add DIY chords. Discuss (a) whether the tune is major, minor or modal, (b) the unusual time, (c) why D₇ may not substitute for D, (d) the slur, (e) why 'to-ry' has only one note.

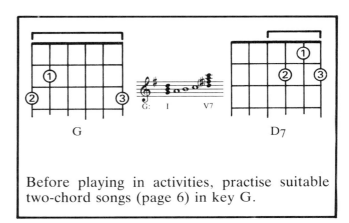

Before playing in activities, practise suitable two-chord songs (page 6) in key G.

Concordant and discordant

This song, also using only chord notes, tells a story (BALLAD). These and 'protest' songs were a means of communication before popular newspapers, radio and television. Early in the nineteenth century the women and young boys worked at the factory power looms. Weekly wages as low as five shillings (25p) caused many men to work at home on hand looms. The song on page 48 shows that the imagination of the Romantic poets was often equally sad!

'The Weaver and the Factory Maid'

Most music does not consist entirely of CONCORDANT (CONSONANT) notes that match each chord. DISCORDANT (DISSONANT) notes are included that 'disagree' with them. In this song there are clashes between the RH (e.g. X), voice (e.g. Y) and the LH double drone.

Schubert's song is the last of a series (SONG CYCLE) about a rejected lover wandering through snowy wastes. He begs companionship from a hurdy-gurdy ('organ') player. The descriptive accompaniment is typical of nineteenth-century lieder (songs):

A song from _Winter's Journey_: 'The Organ Man' **Schubert**

(a) First identify the different near-ostinato interludes in this song. During a recording (in German?), match each interlude with one of the above. Does the song change key? Discuss (i) how the music is made 'bleak', (ii) the interpretation of dynamics/ornament.

Things to do

21. Perform the song sung/on recorder with any glockenspiel playing the drone. Hear bars 1–9 on the piano with a pause at each clash.

22. Write protest song words, improvising a tune with discords as you experiment with chords D, C and G in various orders. Make it modal—begin/end on chord D. Try to write them down. Hear them with guitar/piano.

23. Turn to the song on page 41. Identify all the notes dissonant with the harmony.

24. Rewrite bars 1–5 of Theme A (page 44) in 2/4 time, grouping correctly. Which major key requires a four-sharp key-signature?

25. In previous songs try to find an example of a weak syllable on a strong beat.

11 BACK TO SQUARE ONE

Key E major

Have you noticed that the dominant of each scale is the tonic of the scale with one more sharp? To find the four-sharp key, just go up in perfect 5ths from C:

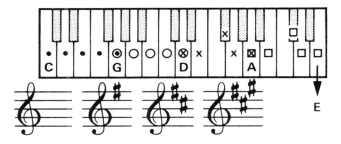

Notice that each key signature includes all previous sharps—and one new one. This is always the seventh degree (leading note) of the scale:

The E major key signature therefore adds D# to the three sharps required by A:

Now look at it another way. The second half of the C major scale is the first half of G major. Similarly, the second half of the G major scale is the first half of D major, and so on:

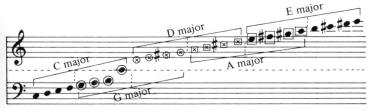

This key sequence is un-altered by inverting some 5ths into 4ths:

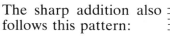

The sharp addition also follows this pattern:

Of course, major scales can always be worked out by stepping out the T and ST pattern: Using one of each letter from E gives F#, not G♭!

Things to do

1. Take/share a chromatic classroom instrument/piano. Play the scales of C, G, D, A and E.
2. Sketch a keyboard and place ● on the keys to show E major. Overlap and continue with O to similarly indicate B major. Add letter names for this (*one* of each). Check the sharps with the rising fifths system. Play as in 1. What is different about the start of the six# major scale?

As the fifth degree of E major is B, then B must be the five-sharp key. The fifth # will be A, its seventh degree. The fifth degree of B major, however, is a 'black' note for the first time. Therefore, in order to keep to the pattern of perfect 5ths, the six-sharp major key must be F# (not F) major. In any case, you already know that F major has one flat!

Key B♭ major

So, scales may start from 'black' notes. Indeed, all keys 'sharper' than B begin on sharps. Now study a reversal of the rising 5ths pattern. Think of it as five notes *down* each scale (also a perfect 5th). Sharps are subtracted—instead of added. After C, added flats equal minus sharps:

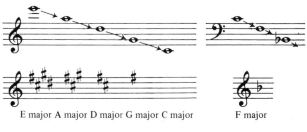

E major A major D major G major C major   F major

Five degrees down the F scale is B♭—the two-flat key. Again you could have worked it out by stepping out the T and ST pattern.

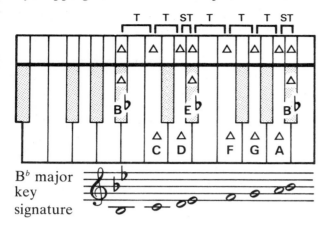

B♭ major key signature

Continuing down, each 5th drop lands on a flat. So, all flat keys beyond F begin on flats.

Again, it is convenient to invert some 5ths into 4ths:

As with sharp keys, each added flat copies the pattern:

If the E major and B♭ major scales are mixed, an interesting thing happens:

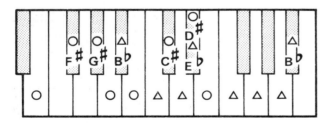

Although D♯ and E♭ are the same on the piano, you cannot swop them.

In E major, the D♯ replaces D♮. Calling it E♭ would give the scale two Es—and also make it look odd:

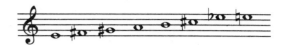

Giving the same note another name is called an ENHARMONIC CHANGE.

In your notebook

(i) Set out and label the key signatures of B♭, F, C, G, D, A and E majors (on both staves).
(ii) Explain enharmonic change. Give examples.

Things to do

3. Rewrite these major key bars with the correct key signature instead of accidentals:

(a)   (b)   (c)

4. Similarly rewrite these, which are in minor keys. Will accidentals still be necessary?

(a)   (b)

(c)

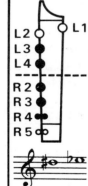

L2 L1
L3
L4

R2
R3
R4
R5

The next recorder note will enable you to play in keys B♭ major and E major/minor. Think of its fingering as 'all on except top and bottom'.

Descant (tenor) players practise (a) the E major scale in different rhythms, (b) the B♭ major scale up to F.

Treble players practise (c) the A major scale down to E (using descant E major fingering—a perfect 4th below). Remember, this will also be the lower half of E major. (d) The complete B♭ major scale (using descant F major fingering).

Stepping parts based on these appear shortly.

50

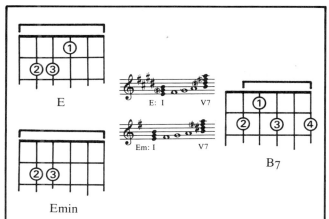

E

Emin

B7

E: I   V7

Em: I   V7

The new chord, B_7, is $V_{(7)}$ in E maj/min. Practise $V_{(7)}$-I in Keys E, A, D maj/min. Strum or use finger-picking styles. E.g. on beat 1, pluck (thumb) the root on the lowest string used (bass). Fingers 1, 2, 3 then pluck strings 3, 2, 1 singly/together in appropriate combinations. In long chords alternate root and 5th/3rd in the bass.

Things to do

5. Play 4 and 5, (i) as written, (ii) as rewritten.
6. Play Theme C (page 44). Rewrite Theme G an octave higher and also play it.
7. In groups, assemble instruments to play DIY chords I and V in E major. Choose a page 6 song. Accompany your singing/piano. Later change chords 'by ear'.
8. Repeat 7 in E minor. Which note is changed?
9. Practise the next song/parts. The cello (bass) part requires stopped strings. This may also be sung to 'la' by any broken voices. Why is the last bar incomplete?

The following song was composed by the nineteenth-century American song-writer, Stephen Foster. His other songs, 'Swannee River' and 'My Old Kentucky Home', describe the life of the American South before the Civil War.

'Camptown Races'   **Stephen Foster**

The key cycle

Turn to page 49. The series of ascending perfect 5ths eventually returns full circle to C again. Descending perfect 5ths (or rising 4ths) cover the same ground in reverse:

The complete major key system may therefore be written as a CIRCLE OF FIFTHS known as THE KEY CYCLE:

Crossing the 'bicycle fork' introduces black note keys. 'White' one way round is 'black' the other—and vice versa. The letters either side of this also start off each key signature sequence:

The sharps add on clockwise from F (two places behind the key). The flats add on anticlockwise from B (one place before the key).
(The number of letters in the words 'sharp' and 'flat' remind us of 5th and 4th respectively.)
The order of # and bs in a key signature can also be remembered by this mnemonic:

→ (rising 5ths)   ←b
Forty Cats Go Down An Empty Barrel
or, if you prefer to reverse the order:

b → (rising 4ths)   ←#
Brown Earth And Damp Grass Cause Fungus

These can also be used like the key cycle. Start from C as before. Remember that the jump to the other end marks the start of 'black' keys.

Things to do

10. Discuss (a) which scales sound identical (enharmonic), (b) the key signature relationship of # and b keys with the same letter, (c) whether a # or b can ever be 'white', (d) whether the order of #s or bs in a signature is the order they are played in a scale, (e) other mnemonics.

11. Use the E major scale (page 49) to help you write out its relative (harmonic) minor scale.
12. Add ×s to a keyboard sketch (as 2) to show the scale of A^b. Check bs with the key cycle.
13. Which keys have (a) five #s, (b) five bs?
14. Compare D$^#$/E^b heard after an (a) E, (b) E^b chord. Discuss 'magnetic' and 'static' effects. Similarly compare singing C – D$^#$/E^b after (c) Em, (d) Cm chords.
15. Is the page 51 song pentatonic? Remove diatonic glockenspiel bars to make it pentatonic in C. Repeat with G and F. What does the pattern remind you of?
16. Draw a keyboard and mark the F$^#$ scale. As its 4th and 7th degrees are the only 'whites', the 'blacks' make F$^#$ pentatonic. Improvise on the 'blacks' in any song rhythm. Combine those in the same time.
17. The music opposite is certainly not pentatonic. Name the modulations at X, Y and Z:

Trio (Scherzo and Trio) from Octet in F, Op. 166:   Schubert

(a) First hear the fast 3/4 Scherzo, scored as for the Trio (overleaf). Explain 'octet' and translate the scoring. The two sections are each repeated. Identify solo wind instruments.
(b) Hear the Trio, following the music. Again there are two repeated sections. Notice:
(i) 'marking time' crotchets in the cello part;
(ii) which wind instrument enters at bar 12;
(iii) in which blank bar the remaining strings enter. Follow the clarinet from this point;
(iv) the double bass entry at bar 53;
(v) whether the dynamics are obeyed.

Related keys

Key signatures identify keys another way:

The last sharp is the leading note. Therefore key E (or C# minor):

The penultimate *b* is the keynote. Therefore key A*b* (or F minor):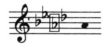
Three clues decide the major/minor question. Apply them to the Trio:
(a) Most pieces begin on the tonic or dominant chord;
(b) The last chord should be the tonic;
(c) Minor key leading note accidentals.
However, much music modulates to other keys before returning home to the tonic.

The most likely modulations are to:
(i) the keys either side in the cycle—the clockwise DOMINANT KEY (five degrees up), with one more # (or one less *b*) and the anti-clockwise SUBDOMINANT KEY (five degrees down=four degrees up) with one more *b* (or one less #)
(ii) the relative minor/major keys of the tonic, dominant and subdominant keys.

All these, with signatures no more than one # or *b* different from the tonic, are called RELATED KEYS. Any modulation is a temporary change of home. Related ones are gentle in effect. However, if you stay away too long there is the danger of regarding it as your real home (tonic key)! Modulations to unrelated keys are usually pleasant surprises. A quick visit to a 'relative' and back is also called a TRANSITION.

Both kinds of modulation occur in the Trio. Notice also: Accidentals are used for short stays in other keys—not new key signatures. The

clarinet and horn transpose, and so do not 'speak the truth'.

The bassoon part, when high, uses the TENOR CLEF:

Compare middle C's position on the viola clef:

(c) Hear just the Scherzo again. Compare the smooth related key modulations in A with the shock of unrelated keys in B. Sections A and B end respectively in the dominant and tonic keys. What are they?
(d) Hear the Trio. Again compare related key modulations in A and generally more distant ones in B.
(e) Now hear the complete movement. Discuss (i) what Scherzo DC means. What is the form of (ii) the complete movement, (iii) the Scherzo, (iv) the Trio? Write down the predominant one-bar rhythm of the Scherzo.

Things to do

18. Discuss (a) why the Octet is 'chamber music', (b) the names of works for three, four, five, six and seven solo instruments. The Scherzo (and Trio) is the third of six movements. What has been the most usual number of movements since the Classical period? Translate all score abbreviations.
19. What is the Trio's tonic key? Discuss (a) the clues, (b) which instruments could fool you. List its five related keys. Do they include the modulations at X, Y and Z? Are the distant modulations in B more in the # or the *b* direction? Why are they called 'distant'? In what way are the keys at the end of A and B similar in both Scherzo and Trio? A transition to D minor occurs in bars 58/9. Why is a mixture of #s and *b*s always a minor key?
20. Write out bars 53–60 of the bassoon part on the bass stave, and bars 1–20 of the viola part on the treble stave. Suggest (a) why the tenor clef was used, (b) why the tenor and alto clefs are so-called.
21. Play the violin I and II parts of the A section. What pleasant interval do they usually make with each other? Which part has an anacrusis? How does this affect the bar numbering? Add the viola part, written as in 20.
22. Identify the tonic keys of songs/hymns.

12 THE THREE-CHORD TRICK

Primary chords (major)

'Camptown Races', on page 51 requires just three chords:

In key E major these are:

In any key, the tonic, subdominant and dominant chords are known as the PRIMARY CHORDS (TRIADS). In major keys, each primary chord is major.

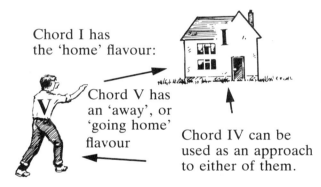

Chord I has the 'home' flavour:

Chord V has an 'away', or 'going home' flavour

Chord IV can be used as an approach to either of them.

Don't forget, any given chord can be in more than one key. In other keys, it will have a different number—and a different effect ('flavour').

For example, in key A major the primary chords:

also have the above primary chord flavours. This means that although the chord of E major has a 'home' flavour in key E, it magically changes its flavour to 'away' when in key A. And so on.

Many songs can be harmonised using just the primary chords. They include:

'Swannee River'   'Tavern in the Town'
'Ten Green Bottles'   'Lord of the Dance'
'Sing Low, Sweet   'Silent Night'
  Chariot'
'She'll be coming round the Mountain'

Things to do

1. First get used to the 'flavour' of chords E, A and B$_{(7)}$ in relation to E major. Now write down I, IV or V as ten such chords are played. Don't be fooled by any repetition of the same chord with different 'second helpings' or in a different arrangement.
2. Listen to 'Camptown Races' (without music) played with a pause at every chord change. Write the chord numbers in the correct order.
3. Repeat 1 in different major keys.
4. Write out the full words of one of the songs given above. Hear it as in 2. Add I, IV or V under the words at the appropriate place. Repeat with other songs/keys. Compare the last two chords of each song.
5. In groups, assemble instruments to play DIY chords I, IV and V in E or A major. Add a double bass/cello (stopping strings if necessary) as a bass. Accompany a song sung by one or more group members. If it is too high/low, change the song/key. Perform to the class.
6. Sing/play 'Camptown Races' (page 51). Add DIY chords to the accompaniment.

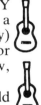

Cadences

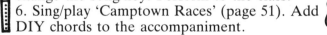

Turn to page 51. All the phrases in 'Camptown Races' are four bars long. Although a phrase can be of any length, you will remember that four (or two) bars is normal—for much simple music at any rate. You can also think of each pair of phrases as one sentence, and of the complete song as one paragraph.

The last two chords of any phrase are particularly important. Called the CADENCE, they have the same effect as punctuation in ordinary language.

The final cadence of most songs including 'Camptown Races' and most

normal music is $V_{(7)} \to I$

This ending, called a   PERFECT CADENCE
                         (FULL CLOSE)

has the effect of   a full stop ●

Full stops not only occur at the very end of stories and poems. In 'Camptown Races' there is also a full stop (perfect cadence) at the end of the second phrase.

The song's third phrase

ends with $IV \to I$

This ending, called a   PLAGAL (AMEN)
                         CADENCE

also has the effect of   a full stop ●

A plagal cadence sounds particularly final when heard after a perfect one—for example, when an Amen is sung at the end of a hymn.

Very often a composer wants a less definite end to a phrase.

In 'Camptown Races',
the first phrase ends on $\to V$

Called an   IMPERFECT
                         CADENCE (HALF
this has the   CLOSE)

unfinished effect of   a comma ,
(whatever the previous chord).

Finally, especially in longer pieces, a composer may want to give you a surprise. He may lead you to expect a perfect cadence. Instead, an unexpected

chord follows V $V \to$ (Not I)

Called an   INTERRUPTED
                         (SURPRISE)
                         CADENCE

this has the effect
of an exclamation or question mark **!?**

These are the most commonly used cadences. However, any two chords that sound pleasant next to each other can be used to end a phrase. Remember also:

(a) A cadence is as much to do with rhythm as chords, and only occurs at the end of a phrase. For example, chords V→I at the beginning or in the middle of a phrase are *not* a perfect cadence.

(b) There can be any number of chords in a phrase.

(c) Primary chords and cadences can occur in all types of vocal and instrumental music.

Things to do

7. Identify the final cadences of the songs on pages 8, 12 and 29 and keys/cadences at the end of each section of the Trio on page 53.

8. Listen to 'Camptown Races' harmonised, with a pause at every cadence. Notice:
(a) imperfect cadences that make the music want to go on;
(b) each perfect/plagal cadence could be the end.

Discuss why this is so.

Repeat, with all the perfect cadences changed to interrupted. It is much more necessary for a melody to end on the true tonic chord than on the tonic note.

9. Also identify the cadences as a selection of the three-chord songs is played in E major. Some of the perfect cadences may be replaced by interrupted ones. Repeat with others in different keys. Listen to an Amen (plagal cadence) added to some of them.

10. Choose an instrument and compose a melody for it using one of these plans. Write in key A or E and in any time, adding the signatures. Use only notes concordant with the harmony, no jumps further than a fifth, and end on a long note. Write only rhythms you can read and notes you can play:

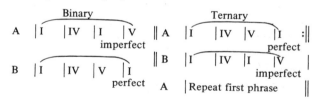

Vote as each is harmonised on the piano.

11. In groups, the composer play the tune and the others DIY chords and a bass part on any suitable instrument. Perform to the class.

12. Write out the scale of B^b major on the treble stave with correct key signature. What is its relative minor key? Now write the primary triads of B^b, using accidentals instead of a key signature. Name each chord—B^b, etc. Notice that chords (like scales) may start on 'black' notes.

13. Accompany the next extract with the parts/ DIY chords. Discuss (a) its phrase lengths, (b) its cadences, (c) where the bass or melody is dissonant with the chord on the beat, (d) the figures over the RH, (e) the Italian terms. Hear the extract played slowly, with a pause at each cadence. Notice (f) syncopation in bar 6, etc., (g) the clashes discussed at (c).

This extract also uses just the primary chords. The mazurka, like the polonaise was a national dance of Chopin's beloved Poland. He wrote over fifty of them. The dotted rhythms and accents/long notes on the second beat are a feature of most mazurkas. Notice also the small ornamental notes, common in Chopin. It is also appropriate to perform Romantic music of this type with little changes of speed—called RUBATO:

The opening of Mazurka in B^b, Op. 7, No. 1:   **Chopin**

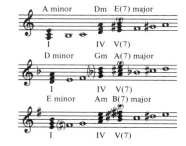

(a) Listen to the complete mazurka. Count the times the above extract returns, following the music each time. In the middle, look out for a sudden modulation and an unusual 'oriental'-sounding section over a LH drone. Identify melodic sequences in the extract. Why are they inexact? Compare different interpretations of tempo, rubato, dynamics, ornaments.

(b) Listen to examples of interrupted cadences from Bach/Handel to modern pop/show music.

In your notebook

(i) Copy or summarise the given descriptions of (a) primary chords, (b) the four cadences.

Primary chords (minor)

Primary chords/cadences also occur in minor keys with the same effects. Compare the primary chords of A major (page 55) and A minor (TONIC MAJOR and TONIC MINOR keys) Notice: (a) Chords I and IV are major/minor to match their keys—and help give the happy/sad sound; (b) The minor key's accidental ensures that both major and minor key Vs are major.

The primary chords in keys:

A minor:

D minor:

E minor:

So, major chords/intervals can occur in a minor key (and minor chords/intervals in a major key). Now similarly compare the tonic major and minor primary chords of keys D and E.

Don't be fooled into thinking that a # or a # key necessarily means a major chord/key:

A # can squash as well as stretch any intervals.

Similarly, a *b* does not necessarily mean minor! A change from tonic major to tonic minor, and vice versa, is not a change of key (home) but a CHANGE OF MODE (Activities 14–16).

Things to do

14. Repeat 1, 2, 4 and 10 in E minor.
15. Rewrite the three melodic parts and chords of the page 51 song in E min. Perform.
16. Repeat 5 in E and A minor. The chords will help you sing the tunes in the minor.
17. Identify short extracts as major/minor.

See the mode change in the music below. The G minor phrase is repeated in the major. Like all minors, the relationship between G minor and its relative major is as follows:

Similarly, any relative major is found by going three degrees up the minor scale. Unfortunately, in a vicious circle, one does not know whether that note is a #, *b* or ♮ until the (relative major's) key signature is found!

Instead, think of the relative major as being a minor 3rd up any minor scale. So, go up the tonic major scale to find the major third. Then lower a semitone. Some musicians work out a minor 3rd by counting three semitones.

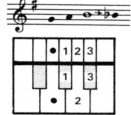

The tonic minor always has three more *b*s (or three less #s) than its tonic major key:

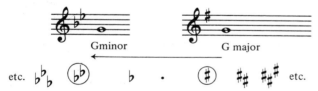

Here are the primary chords of G minor:

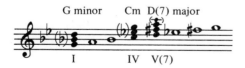

Things to do

18. Count/clap the Dvorak opening (a) without, (b) with ties. In two groups clap 3/4 against the given 3/2 3/4 3/4 ostinato. Notice syncopation. Discuss why one 3/2 'bar' equals two 3/4 bars.
19. Play the opening as in 18 (a) and (b). Compare the minor/major mode flavour of each half.
20. Play DIY chords I and V in G major and minor. Which chord is unaltered? Repeat 19 slowly, adding the chords as indicated. Why could the minor 3rd = three semitones method lead to error?
21. Rewrite Theme B (page 35) in G minor, and the upper part of Theme F (page 44) an 8ve lower in G major and minor. Play each version.

(c) Hear the following work. It is in ternary form: A B A with a contrasted quiet B section. Count the times the given theme appears in each A section. Do not be fooled by tunes in a similar rhythm. Identify:
(i) orchestration changes in these repeats;
(ii) the solo instrument(s) featured in B;
(iii) the coda (the A sections are identical).

In the coda, notice modulations, a hint of B and a sudden final loud return of half the extract. Is it in G major or minor? During a third playing, clap or play the ostinato in the A sections.
(d) Continue Smetana's 'Vlatava' (page 35);
(iv) a soft wind chord build-up, then flutes almost as in (i) over a slow violin tune. The brass enter *ppp*. A crescendo leads to
(v) Theme A. When it changes to the major mode, prepare for an *ff* interrupted cadence
(vi) brass fanfares, violin scales and the piccolo. A diminuendo and key change usher in
(vii) Theme A *ff* in the major mode (the river flows through Prague). Soon, in the coda, repeated *ff* perfect cadences herald the end. Next, rhythmic repetitions of Chord I lead to a diminuendo on a rising/falling broken chord. An *ff* staccato perfect cadence ends the work. Many long pieces end with (V) I repetitions.

The opening of Slavonic Dance in G min, Op. 46, No. 8   **Dvorak**

13 LIES AND STORIES

Instruments in F, B♭, A

Things to do

1. Rewrite 'Go Tell Aunt Mary' (page 36) in keys (a) D major, (b) E major, (c) E minor. Play/sing and accompany each version with DIY I, V chords. Discuss mode change, transposition, and modulation.

Now find and listen to the other examples at (i), (ii) and (iii) below (played on the piano).

It is easy to confuse these terms. Remember:
  (i) *Mode change* involves modifications in a tune's melody and harmony (as in 1(a) (b)). See also Schumann extracts B and F (page 38) and Dvorak extract (page 58).
  (ii) *Transposition* repeats a tune exactly—at a higher or lower pitch (as in 1(c)).
  (iii) *Modulation* is any change of key (major or minor) during a piece. Transposition necessitates modulation. See 'America' (page 73)

Remember, some instruments transpose automatically. Those commonly used are:

Horn in F   *Cor Ánglais*

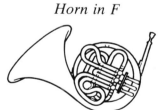 

With these, as C fingering produces F, a perfect 5th lower:

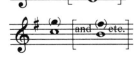

parts are written a perfect 5th higher, and in the key a perfect 5th higher:

Because of the Circle of Fifths, this key will always have one more # (or one less b). However, horn parts are usually written with accidentals not signatures:

Instruments in B♭

B♭ clarinet   *B♭ trumpet*

 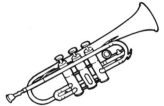

With these, as C fingering produces B♭, a major 2nd (tone) lower:

parts must be written a tone higher and in a key a tone higher:

The Circle of Fifths shows why this key always has two more #s (or two less bs)), e.g.

On score instrument lists the b is often omitted. The bass clarinet (in B♭) sounds a further octave below the above :

Instruments in A

A clarinet   *A trumpet*

With these, as C fingering produces A, a minor 3rd lower:

parts must be written a minor 3rd higher. Think about why this key will always have three more bs (see page 58).

Remember transposing instruments always tell lies!

59

Things to do

2. Rewrite the Slavonic Dance opening (page 58) as a part for B^b clarinet. Play both versions. Discuss which rule is obeyed by the key signature changes here and in 1(a-c).
3. Rewrite the last eight bars of the clarinet and horn parts (page 53) as they would sound.

In your notebook

(i) (Copy, unjumbling the words)
Snap sorting instruments sound notes different from those *tin trew*. *Clear nits* and *pert muts* in B^b and the *rhon* in F are the most common.

Orchestration

Several transposing instruments appear in the following score. The music and dancing of Tchaikovsky's *Nutcracker Suite* illustrates a girl's dream. In it, a nutcracker and other objects come to life.

In concerts, only a selection (suite) of the movements is played. In the movement shown, Tchaikovsky's *Nutcracker Suite* illustrate a girl's dream. In it, a nutcracker and other objects come to life.

Also find the following new orchestral terms:

DIV(ISI)	The sub-division of a string section into two or more groups (instead of double stopping, etc), bar 17.
1(2)	Only the 1st (or 2nd) of two players to play, e.g. bar 16. (A^2 or 3u2 means both play again).
SOLO	An important part for one player.

But all parts are important really, the accompaniment as well as the melody. None can be left out as each has a job to do. These include:
Main Melody: e.g. celesta, bars 5–16.
Secondary Melody (Countermelody, obbligato): e.g. bass clarinet, bars 8–11.
Doubling: e.g. flutes 'shadow' celesta an 8ve lower, bars 17–19.
Bass Parts: the lowest part(s) sounding.
Harmony: parts completing or strengthening the chords, e.g. upper strings, bars 1–16.
Holding Notes: making the harmony more 'solid', e.g. bass clarinet, bars 13–16.
Rhythm: e.g. strings, bars 1–16.
Sometimes a part does more than one job at a time. In orchestration, many parts frequently change jobs. Notice all these musical devices:
Sequence: bars 17–20, esp. celesta part.
Imitation: between clarinets I/II, bars 16–18.
PEDAL (POINT): a continuous (drone) or repeated note (tonic or dominant), usually in the bass, e.g. cello/bass, bars 1–8.

The harmony of the other parts is often dissonant with it. DOUBLE PEDALS (two-note drones) are also possible. You can see why pedals are frequent in organ music!

Opening of 'Sugar Plum Fairy' (*Nutcracker Suite*)

Tchaikovsky

(a) First listen to the music overleaf, stopping at the end of bar 17. Follow the pizz. strings, jumping to the celesta (bar 5), the bass clarinet (bar 8), back to the celesta (bar 13), clarinet (bar 16), celesta (bar 17). Guess how the sequence is going to continue. Discuss the job(s) done throughout by each part.

Now listen to the complete movement. In section (A) opposite, did you guess right after bar 17? Is the clarinet imitation or the celesta part the main melody here?

In the next section (B) notice a two-bar clarinet/celesta phrase followed by the cor anglais/violins. This is repeated. A rising clarinet/celesta sequence leads to a solo celesta passage of rising arpeggios. A short descending wind scale leading to a repeat of the A section.

As you follow the above again, notice (i) changes in orchestration. Now discuss (ii) the movement's form, (iii) the tonic key, (iv) the notes played at X. The sequence in bars 17–19 modulates. It is based on three perfect cadences in different keys. What are they?

Now compare bars 5–8 with 13–16. Which string parts are syncopated?

After discussing the meaning of all the signs and Italian terms/abbreviations printed in the extract, listen to it again. Discuss (v) whether they are all obeyed, (vi) possible improvements in the interpretation.

(b) from the same ballet, hear the 'Chinese Dance', all written above a pizz. double bass pedal on B^b. Listen for (i) four flute phrases separated by pizz. strings, the last two joined by the piccolo, (ii) two more similar flute/piccolo phrases now accompanied by fast clarinet tonic and dominant broken chords. These then continue to the end.

(c) Now hear 'Dance of The Toy Flutes', a ternary (ABA) piece in D major. In A, listen for: (i) flutes above pizz. strings. A repeat of this tune ends with a rising sequence. The cor anglais then joins the flutes; (ii) a repeat of the main theme, more fully orchestrated; (iii) section B, in the mediant minor, consisting entirely of repetitions of a four-bar ostinato. Name the key. Identify the instrument(s) first playing the theme and accompaniment. Which new families join after eight bars? Which percussion instrument, plays 'off beat' throughout? Quiet flutes lead to the return of A, without the repeat. Can you tell which instrument(s) has a countermelody now?

Things to do

4. Write bars 8–11 of the bass clarinet part (bass stave) and bars 16–17 of the clarinet part, both as sounding. Discuss (a) why B^b instruments are more suitable for flat keys, (b) why all instruments are not made at concert pitch.
5. Discuss each part's job(s) in the given score. Find modulation, (tonic) pedal, sequence, imitation. Now find sequences on pages 12, 25 and 53 and double pedals elsewhere.

A ballet score is Programme Music. Although the dancing, acting and scenery make the story clear, the music also suits the action or mood. Most Programme Music, however aims to make us think of 'something else' (e.g. story, person, animals, place, time of day, mood) using just music. The orchestra can often approximate natural or man-made sounds. However, it is much more difficult with things like 'sunset' or 'fear'. There is also nothing to stop 'storm' music being imagined as a lion or anger. But composers have a large 'paint box' to choose from:

Different Instrument(s)/Orchestration: see page 60

Musical Material: key/mode modulations, harmony, cadences, pitch, intervals, broken chords, scales, musical devices, time/rhythm.

Performing Method/Style: tempo, volume, dynamics, staccato, legato, etc.

(d) Hear 'The Carnival of The Animals' (without Finale) by Saint Saens (France). It depicts (not in order): fish, pianists, lion, fossils, elephant, swan, donkeys, birds, chickens, asses, tortoise, cuckoo, kangeroos. List in the correct order. Repeat (i) noting which clues from the above lists helped you, (ii) which items briefly reappear in the Finale. Discuss other 'programmes' the music suggests (e.g. events, moods).

(e) Treat Programme pieces/Tone Poems as (d).

Things to do

6. List/discuss items from the above 'paint box' for suggesting in music: romance, rain, duck, war, fear, humour, horse, UFO, night. What is (a) easiest/hardest to depict, (b) the difference between 'word painting' and Programme Music?

The easiest way to tell a story in music is to sing it—as in an opera. Some of the greatest Romantic operas are by Richard Wagner. The bridal march ('Here comes the bride') played at weddings, comes from *Lohengrin*. The later operas, called music dramas, include the *Ring* cycle of four works. These were designed to be heard on four successive evenings—about fifteen hours of music! The story, involving dwarfs, giants and gods, concerns gold stolen from the Rhine and hammered into a magic ring.

They are examples of GRAND OPERA. He also wrote the words (LIBRETTO). At about the same time, in England, Gilbert and Sullivan were writing their popular light or COMIC OPERAS.

(f) Hear the final scene from 'Twilight of the Gods', the last of Wagner's *Ring* operas. The magic ring has brought final ruin. The Rhine overflows, the ring is returned to it and Valhalla, the home of the gods, goes up in flames. Notice (a) how continuous the music is, with few cadence stops, (b) how the orchestra illustrates the final disaster, (c) the concluding 'Romantic' string tune.

(g) Now hear a Gilbert and Sullivan extract.

The Tchaikovsky and Wagner works above show some of the later nineteenth-century trends. More expression and musical emotion required:
Larger orchestra/choirs and new instruments
Greater contrasts in volume and tempo
More modulations to unrelated keys
An increased use of CHROMATIC notes. These are non-diatonic notes that add 'colour' to a key without causing a modulation.

But bigger/louder does not necessarily mean better! Debussy (France) developed new ideas —for example, music based on unusual scales such as the pentatonic. Here it is in F: He also used the whole-tone scale. Here it is from F.

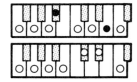

This scale sounds 'homeless', as it has no semitone to lead anywhere. It also sounds vague, as all the intervals are the same. This is true of the chromatic scale featured in the following. Less emphasis on regular beats/rhythms increases the dreamy static effect of much Debussy.

Opening flute theme from *Prelude à l'après-midi d'un Faune*   Debussy

(h) First get used to the music's flavour by hearing the given whole-tone scale and flute theme on the piano. Discuss the title. The work mainly consists of varied repetitions/fragments of this theme. Follow its first five appearances on the flute. Clarinet 'waves' over muted horns lead into a whole-tone scale—up and down, echoed by the flute at a different pitch. Another clarinet 'wave' and the scales are repeated. As the music continues (ii) identify prominent instruments when requested.

Which unusual instruments provide some of the harmony and 'colour'? During the quiet ending, notice two pitched antique cymbals. Try to beat time when a section is repeated!

Debussy did not set out to make this normal 'Programme' music—although it later became a ballet. Like the French painters of his time, he was more interested in *suggesting* ideas and making an *impression*. What is your impression?

Things to do

7. Write out the chromatic scale portions of the above. Play the whole extract (making enharmonic changes). Why is it strictly incorrect to refer to 'diatonic' and 'chromatic' glockenspiels?

8. Discuss why pentatonic tunes (a) are easy to write, (b) mix pleasantly. What have the pentatonic sales of C, F and G in common? Which pentatonic scale is all 'black'? Now combine pentatonic ostinati in one of these keys. They could be in the rhythm of song phrases in the same time.

9. Write/play a four-phrase pentatonic melody in G. Include only notes and rhythms you can play and no interval greater than an octave.

10. Assemble chime bars for the whole tone scale opposite. Using it, either (a) compose/improvise a melody, (b) in groups, combine improvised ostinati. What have the pentatonic and whole-time scales in common? Why does the former sound more 'normal'?

14 THE TWENTIETH CENTURY

Although composers had generally done 'more of their own thing' in the nineteenth century, they still stuck to the major and minor scale system when constructing their tunes and chords. These had been in fashion since the Baroque period. The twentieth century, however, has been a period of change, variety and experiment. Very few composers today write like any others. There is, therefore, no such thing as a single twentieth-century style in music—or in any of the other arts.

Many believe that 'modern music' started with Debussy late in the nineteenth century. He and others disliked the exaggeration of late Romantic music. Some also felt that the addition of a lot of 'wrong-note' chromatic decoration to the basic scales made them lose their character. In a similar way, simple buildings can be spoilt by too much colour or by sticking on too many ornamental features. Many composers also began to think that the old scales had been used up in any case. It was becoming increasingly difficult to write a major key tune that did not sound like somebody else's!

However, modern trends in all the arts are probably mostly due to the feelings many people have about life today. We live in a world dominated by dissatisfaction, despair, rebellion and a rejection of past standards and values. Just consider what you see on the average television news programme!

When the past is rejected, men have to invent their own systems. This is what has happened in music. The twentieth century has also seen the return of British composers to the 'First Division'.

Tonal, atonal and microtonal music

Music based on some major or minor scale and with a 'home' note and chord is said to be

TONAL. Most of the new systems invented have no such basis, every note of the chromatic scale being considered of equal importance. 'Democratic' music of this type, without important 'home' notes to remember and end on, is called ATONAL.

The first composer to experiment with atonal music was the Austrian, Arnold Schoenberg. At first he allowed himself the luxury of being able to use all the semitones in any order. Perhaps you think it is easy to write tunes and chords where anything goes? But a world without rules means that nothing is right or wrong. There has also been an interest in intervals smaller than a semitone. MICROTONAL music is common in some Oriental cultures.

Edward VII   Edward VIII
George V   George VI
SUFFRAGETTES   Elizabeth II
WORLD WAR I
RUSSIAN REVOLUTION
Wright Brothers   Atomic Bomb
WORLD WAR II
FILMS   MOON-LANDING
RADIO
TELEVISION

Serial music

So, it was not long before Schoenberg and his pupils Alban Berg and Anton Webern invented their own rules. Their music became based on the twelve notes of the chromatic scale arranged in some fixed order. This SERIES or TONE ROW was different for each piece. The tunes and harmony had to be based on this fixed order of notes—in any rhythm. The series could be repeated, transposed, reversed, have its intervals inverted, combined and so on. Many later composers have turned to SERIALISM for some of their music. Atonal composers not only abandoned the familiar major/minor sounds. Like Debussy before them, they relied far less on regular beats, times and rhythms.

Electronics

The arrival of the tape recorder and electronic sound generation also stimulated new composing methods. Some composers developed MUSIQUE CONCRÈTE, which is the result of recording, modifying and mixing (synthesising) natural sounds such as a banging door or dripping water. Others similarly used the electronic sounds generated by the apparatus itself. In both cases, the composer could often fix his ideal performance on tape. He was now both composer and performer.

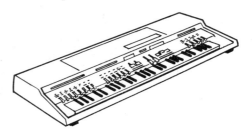

However, do not confuse composition using electronics with electronic imitation of normal instruments or music.

65

Chance

This kind of musical dictatorship was the complete opposite to yet another development in which one or more aspects of a composition or its performance were left to chance. In this 'democratic' ALEATORY music (named after the Latin for dice) the performer(s) are allowed some control over things like choice of notes and when to play them. Thus, no two performances can ever be alike. Irrationality and the effect of chance are also behind some of the trends in modern painting:

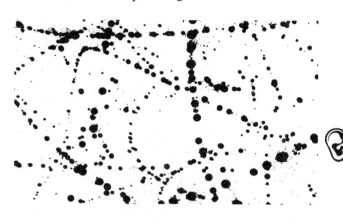

Much experimental music cannot be written in the usual way. New notations have to be invented to enable other people to perform it.

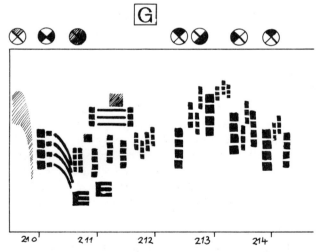

The interest in exotic sounds for their own sake has also led to the introduction of unfamiliar or foreign instruments, or of normal ones played in unusual ways. New titles also have to be invented. You would hardly expect the above to be called a symphony! Now can you see how close your own experimental notation and activities have been to some modern music?

Conservative and neo-classical composers

So-called conservative composers have continued to flourish. These include Edward Elgar, Ralph Vaughan Williams, Benjamin Britten, William Walton and Michael Tippett (Britain), Charles Ives, Aaron Copland and Leonard Bernstein (America) and Serge Prokoviev, Sergei Rachmaninov and Dmitri Shostakovich (Russia). Some have gone back to the rhythms and forms of earlier composers like Bach, while using modern scales and harmony. Among these NEO-CLASSICAL composers are Igor Stravinsky (Russia), Bela Bartok (Hungary) and Paul Hindemith (Germany). Although many of the above tried experimental methods, they have mainly developed the traditional system.

(a) Listen to and compare short extracts of (i) serial, (ii) electronic, (iii) aleatory, (iv) neo-classical, (v) electronic Bach music. After which is it possible to sing a home (tonic) note? Later, identify other extracts in random order.

(b) Hear any recordings of their own music played or conducted by the above composers.

Assignments

(A) Find out which of the composers mentioned above eventually worked in countries other than their own. Briefly summarise their lives.
(B) Although now in the musical 'First Division', Britain still tends to have an inferiority complex. Performers may no longer be tempted to use foreign names, but we can still be falsely impressed by Continental accents and language. List examples from names of shops, food, etc.
(C) Find out the names of present-day makers of the following: pianos, violins, guitars, organs, recorders, wind instruments, brass instruments.
(D) If you use a hymn book with music, find the total of (a) hymn words, (b) hymn tunes written in this century. Compare with the totals of those written in the eighteenth and nineteenth centuries.
(E) In one copy of *The Radio Times* find the proportion of musical works written in the twentieth century.

15 MUSICAL ARITHMETIC

Frequency and harmonics

Things to do

1. In groups, set up a pendulum. Observe the effect on the rate of swing of changing (a) the extent or energy of the initial push, (b) the length of the pendulum.

2. Gently feel the much faster vibrations as available percussion/stringed instruments are hit/plucked. Guess their approximate rate per second.

Every pendulum has its natural speed or FRE-QUENCY, which can only be changed by altering its length.

Similarly, the vibrating parts of musical instruments—or the air inside—also have fixed frequencies. The extremely high musical frequencies, much too fast for the eye to count, are what control pitch. Different instruments (or objects) with the same frequency will therefore have the same pitch.

As with the pendulum, altering the frequency (changing the pitch) is usually done by changing the length of the vibrating part:

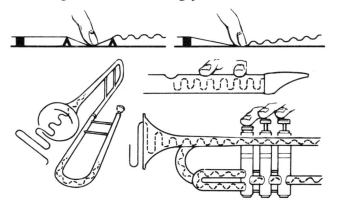

However, the 'fixed' frequencies of keyboard strings and stringed instruments can also be altered (tuned):

Shorter⎫
Tighter⎬ = Faster Vibr./Higher Frequency
         = Higher Pitch

Things to do

3. Assemble pitched percussion, stringed, woodwind and brass instruments. Any players assist in demonstrating (a) open string tuning, (b) the actions involved in playing different notes. Now discuss (c) instruments associated with the above diagrams, (d) fret, peg, valve, piston, slide, finger board, stopping. Finally, suggest how the pitch of a chime bar could be changed, later seeing if your ideas work.

4. Get into groups, each with a stringed instrument. Using finger stopping or a moveable bridge, compare the pitch of each open string with that of (a) half, (b) quarter its vibrating length.

5. Firmly hold the end of a ruler, pencil, etc. and tap the edge of your table. Compare the pitch when hitting (a) the end you are holding, (b) the middle. Explain what happens. Now try playing tunes.

When the vibrating length of a string, bar or the air in a tube is halved

it vibrates at twice the speed and sounds the octave above:

A quarter of this length vibrates four times as fast and sounds two octaves above:

Doubling makes frequencies get high very quickly. Even low piano C has 33 vibrations per second (cycles per sec, cps or hertz). Between 10,000 and 20,000 cps (coming down with age) sounds become inaudible (ULTRASONIC).

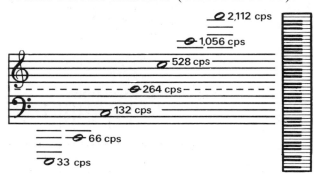

Vibrations are complicated as well as rapid. In addition to the fundamental frequency:

(a)

imagine also a rider sitting in the middle shaking each half at twice this speed:

(b)

Then imagine at the same time (but it cannot be shown!) two riders shaking each third at three times the speed—adding a sound a perfect 5th higher still:

(c)

Then imagine three riders shaking each quarter at four times the fundamental frequency (two octaves higher), and so on! The number of these additional much softer notes, called harmonics, varies between instruments. In fact, it is their presence or otherwise that helps make instruments playing the same note sound different in tone (timbre). Remember also, it is this same harmonic series that brass players can get from just *one* length of tube. Each length of string or tube will produce its own series. Here is the harmonic series from a low C:

String players can play harmonics by preventing the fundamental from vibrating. For example, lightly touching the centre of the string will damp (a) and (c) above and leave the string only free to vibrate in halves (and quarters, etc).

Any harmonic series helps explain why the usual scales and chords sound so normal. The important intervals (perfect 8ve, 5th, major 3rd, minor 3rd) occur first, and the first six harmonics spell out a major chord.

The pitch of any particular note has changed over the years. At present, pianos and orchestral players tune to treble stave A=440c.p.s. (concert pitch). As brass band instruments are often pitched slightly higher, you may have trouble when mixing the two kinds.

Things to do

6. Suggest why strings of the same vibrating length can sound different pitches. Can different-length strings sound the same note? Why do not piano strings double in length for every lower octave?
7. Check the pitch of your piano with a tuning fork. Compare the timbre of different instruments playing the same note (and frequency).
8. Discuss whether there are (a) pitches higher and lower than those on the piano, (b) any

pitches between the fixed piano semitones. Name instruments that could play them. Explain (c) why being slightly out of tune is often worse than playing a wrong note. If the science department has the apparatus, see who can hear the highest pitch. What has this to do with bat's squeaks and police dog whistles?

9. Fix a piece of cardboard on the front fork of an upturned bicycle so that the rotating spokes rub against it. Hear the effect of different speeds. Discuss (a) how to work out the pitch frequency of any given 'pedalling' rate, (b) what you would hear if you could wobble your finger 55 times a second.

10. Work out the frequency of (a) all the As on your piano, (b) both treble stave Es. Why are organ shops often marked 16′, 8′, 4′ and 2′?

11. If the fundamental of a 2ft 'string' is middle C, where must it be 'stopped' to sound

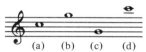

12. Why do the semitone guitar frets gradually get closer? Now listen as an orchestral stringed instrument is plucked, fingering each 'semitone' the same distance as the first one.

13. Write out the first six notes of the harmonic series from

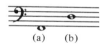

14. Try to get notes from brass instruments (without touching valves, etc). Write each new recognisable pitch on a stave. Compare with the harmonic series patterns and work out the fundamental. Turn to the score on page 14. Discuss why Mozart's brass parts consist of just a few notes. Any recorder players demonstrate how higher harmonics can be produced simply by overblowing. (This is why the upper octave fingering on many instruments is similar to the lower.) If possible, string players demonstrate harmonic playing.

15. Compare and discuss the vibrations of a long horizontally held string/wire/elastic when small weights are fixed dividing it into halves, thirds, quarters, etc. (see opposite page).

16. Bass C will be held on the piano. Listen for each of its lower harmonics in turn (page 68). Repeat with other fundamentals. Discuss why the perfect 5th is important in musical theory.

In your notebook

(i) In your own words, briefly explain frequency, ultrasonic, concert pitch and harmonics.

String scales

The sequence of keys (and the # and b required) is based on rising/falling perfect 5ths (or 4ths). Further, the second most important degree and chord is the dominant (5th), and the related keys are a 5th (or 4th) away from the tonic. Even the open strings of most instruments are tuned a 5th apart.

This enables, for example, the lower and upper halves of scales starting from violin open strings to be played on adjacent strings using similar fingering:

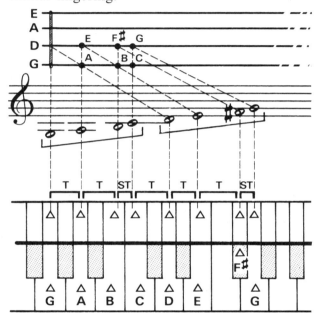

You should now see why orchestral and string works are more often in sharp keys than flat ones. Guitar players are lucky, however. They can make difficult keys easier by using a CAPO. This then makes the guitar a transposing instrument, as the player fingers the chords of one key while sounding a higher one. For example, this capo position will raise the pitch (and key) three semitones (a min. 3rd).

The chords of the page 29 song are now easier.
Just transpose each one
a minor 3rd *down*   (key) F C(7) B♭ Gm
to compensate: (key) D A₇ G Em

Things to do

17. Copy the string scale diagram (without keyboard), but in relation to C major and cello C and G strings with the bass stave. Each half of the scale is TTS. Added together, there is a 'missing' tone. Explain this.

18. Watch the lowest string major scale plucked on a vertically held cello/violin/viola. Nonplayers also have a go—while the rest criticise the tuning (chalk marks may possibly be allowed on the fingerboard). Suggest and then demonstrate how the scale can be played on just one string. Now discuss (a) whether the tone stopping gaps are all the same, (b) why the bass is tuned in 4ths, (c) why beginner string players prefer # keys, (d) the different problems involved in playing scales on the piano and violin.

19. Open the piano. See the TTSTTTS pattern on the hammers as a ruler depresses the C scale.

20. Non-pianists play one finger major scales starting from given 'black' keys. Listen for mistakes and/or watch the hammer pattern.

21. Sing (a) previous two/three-chord songs accompanied by guitar. Repeat, variously raising the key by using a capo. (b), 'Waltzing Matilda' (page 29), in key F adding guitar with Capo as on page 69 (or any alternatives).

Chord progression

The interval of a 5th (or 4th) is also important in harmony. Chord roots jump these intervals up or down in perfect and plagal cadences:

Key C V   I   IV   I

Chords within a phrase also sound satisfying when they jump 4ths/5ths. This progression, common in pre-twentieth century tonal music, is still used in many kinds of popular music today. It often behaves like perfect cadences in various major/minor keys, e.g.:

Amaj/min: V   I Gmaj:V   I

Sometimes the progression is all in one key. This may involve the use of both primary chords (I, IV and V) and SECONDARY CHORDS (II, III and VI). Notice that the secondary chords of a major key are *minor* triads!

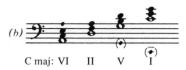

C maj: VI   II   V   I

Notice also that open strings taken one way or the other, match or are 8ves of the above. (a)=bass (or violin), (b)=cello (or viola). Of course, chord roots need not be open strings. The 4ths need not all be perfect either:

Melodic sequences are often based on a rising 4ths (or falling 5ths) chord progression. However, this progression is by no means the only one used in traditional type music. When you compare the following harmonisations of the National Anthem you will hear how effective others are, too:

However, from Debussy onwards, even conservative tonal composers tried to create new effects. They did this not only by inventing new chord mixtures, but also by using the basic triads in unusual relationships.

Things to do

22. One pupil pluck (a) on a bass (violin) as an ostinato. Change note every bar as in rhythms (i), (ii), (iii) or (iv):

Add DIY chords, comparing A maj/min versions.

23. Repeat 22 with (b) using a cello/viola. Which chords are minor? Play again, making one or more of the minor chords major. Recognise which when played on the piano.

24. Treat (c) as a DIY ostinato chord pattern. Which 4th is not perfect? Now discuss why F and B are 'awkward' notes in key C major.

25. Improvise/write a continuous tune to fit one of the above progressions played, once, twice or four times. Use one chord per bar, triad notes, no jumps greater than an 8ve and only notes you can play/sing. Add words. Perform in groups, with DIY chords.

70

26. Compare 22–25, using chords backwards.
27. Compare National Anthem openings (d) and (e). Which chord jump is not a 4th/5th? Identify (i) secondary triads, (ii) minor triads.
28. Hear bars 5–8 of the theme (page 40) on the piano. The rising 4th chords are A(7), Dm, G(7) and C. Accompany with DIY chords. Now turn to page 61. Work out the rising 4th chords of bars 18–19 and add them DIY to the celesta (piano) part. Both extracts are sequences. In what ways is the first one less exact?
29. In groups, arrange DIY chords in any order. Improvise a tune to fit and perform to class.
30. Also in groups, invent new chord mixtures (a) using the notes of one particular scale, (b) using any notes. Arrange different chords in phrases, add a tune (this time not necessarily matching each chord) and perform as in 29.

(a) Listen to 'Four Dance Episodes' from Aaron Copland's ballet *Rodeo*. Although tonal, it sounds quite modern because it includes (a) normal chords in unusual moves, (b) syncopated rhythms, (c) a 'hill-billy' piano, (d) cowboy songs. First read the record sleeve for each movement's 'programme'. Particularly listen for:
'Buckaroo Holiday': syncopation
'Corral Nocturne': unusual opening chord moves
'Saturday Night Waltz: open strings and a familiar tune. Which instrument first plays it?
'Hoe Down': decorated open strings, piano, percussion, a gramophone 'running down' effect. Repeat, discussing how the composer creates the effect of a bucking bronco, wide-open spaces, night-time, a ranch house dance.
(b) Hear the gunfight from Copland's 'Billy the Kid'.
(c) Listen to Variations on 'America' by Charles Ives (USA). Discuss (i) the theme, (ii) how it is varied.
(d) Listen to Prokofiev's 'Classical Symphony'. Its forms/rhythms imitate the Classical style, but its harmony is more modern. Identify prominent instruments and notice sequences and abrupt modulations.
(e) Hear the opening (at least) of the first movement of Rachmaninov's 2nd Piano Concerto. Over a low repeating pedal note, the chords gradually change 'flavour', one note changing each time. The following Romantic violin melody and accompanying piano broken chords make it sound nineteenth century. If possible, hear the composer's own recording.
(f) Listen to pop music with unusual chords.

Serial composition

(a) to (f) are all tonal. The next work is a mixture of tonal and atonal music. During it, tone row B is transposed, inverted and played backwards (RETROGRADE). A Bach chorale also appears—unusually beginning with a whole-tone scale (C).

Extracts from Violin Concerto
Alban Berg

(g) Hear the above. Identify perfect 5ths in A, major/minor 3rds in B. Compare whole-tone notations in B and C. In a recording, notice: Solo open string pattern and continuation (A). The tone row first played in above form (B). (much later) Separate chorale phrases on solo violin (with atonal harmony), woodwind (Bach's harmony as in C), trombone, flutes. High violin harmonics herald the end.
(h) Hear the original chorale (Bach, Cantata 50).
(i) Compare any completely serial piece by Schoenberg. Sing a tonic note! Discuss why it sounds more 'modern' than the Berg.

Things to do

31. Rearrange series B without leger lines (treble stave). List triads made by any three successive notes. Now write it in the rhythm of the first twelve notes of one of the first three tunes of Chapter 9, 12. Play to the class on any instrument.
32. Identify songs as this series (repeated as necessary) is played in their rhythm.
33. Invent your own Tone Row, using one of each of all the semitones, without enharmonic repeats (you could take them out of a hat). Treat as in 31–2. After each performance, sing a tonic! Discuss why this is difficult.
34. Compose a longer serial melody. Use your series repeated, with/without bar lines, retrograde, etc. Write in any rhythm and include rests. Write/combine different atonal melodies. Perform in groups.

16 I'VE GOT RHYTHM

Rhythm in the twentieth century

The twentieth century has seen many developments in rhythm. Some composers have abandoned regular beats and rhythmic patterns altogether. Others, like Stravinsky, have experimented with complicated or frequently changing times/rhythms. The following are among several from Latin America. Unlike many older dances, most modern ones (and pop) are in quadruple time:

Samba: (tambourine) (a)

(bongoes) (b)
Beguine:
(wood block) (c)

These both combine well with each other and with the West Indian calypso rhythm of the next song. It looks as if some notes are 'holding hands' incorrectly. This unusually grouped syncopated 4/4 pattern is common in calypsos:

This grouping: causes the same notes to have a very different effect from: (d)

(e)

Chapter 15, 23 (iv) and (c) above are variations of this Calypso rhythm. So is this:

A different accentuation or note grouping greatly affects music. Exactly the same notes can be made to have a very different effect. E.g.: (f)

This song opening is completely changed if grouped in 3/4 time:

This explains why time signatures may not be treated like fractions:

'Ye Banks and Braes' etc.
(g)
1   2

(h)
1   2   3

$\frac{6}{8}$ does not $= \frac{3}{4}$

Things to do

1. Practise rhythm (d) as an ostinato. Tap a table and another object/instrument with each hand. Try: RLLRLLRL, LRRLRRLR and RLRLRLRL, accenting as shown. Why may this be tricky? Now practise rhythm (f) using RLRLRL. All this should help you now clap similar rhythms. Finally, using contrasted percussion, combine rhythms (a)-(f).
2. Clap the rhythm of the song's bass part. Which of rhythms (a)–(f) is bar 1 basically identical to? See also Chapter 15, 23 (iv).
3. Combine rhythms (d) and (e), exaggerating accents. Which calypso accent is syncopated?
4. Practise the song parts. A triad's fifth is effective in the bass if on an 'after beat'—and convenient when on an adjacent open string. Identify each fifth. Add (i) DIY chords, (ii) ostinati percussion in any (a)–(f) rhythm. When appropriate, use your most natural two-handed method—or play with one hand, (iii) guitars, strumming down/up in rhythm (f). Which song bars clash with this calypso rhythm?
5. Repeat previous 4/4 songs, adding percussion and guitar in the above rhythms.
6. Rewrite the chords and three melodic parts in D minor (the bass is the same). Discuss the problem in bars 1–2 of the song. Perform, without guitar.
7. Without looking, identify (a) each chord as the song (harmonised) is played with suitable pauses, (b) each two-bar phrase cadence.
8. Sing (g) and (h) to 'la'. Compare/combine.
9. Group the times that have the same effect: 4/8, 6/8, 2/2, 3/4, 3/8, 4/4, 6/4, 4/2, 3/2. Suggest why (a) old music, originally written with e.g. semibreve beats has crotchet beats in modern editions, (b) hymn tunes are often printed with minim beats.
10. Recognise tunes (a) from their rhythm, (b) from their notes in the wrong rhythm/time or in the rhythm of another tune. Is (a) easier?
11. Practise these DIY chords, playing (a)–(f) on percussion, once per bar. Add rhythms,

$\frac{4}{4}$ G | Em | A(7) | C | E(7) | B(7) | C | G ‖

Another three-chord song: 'Linstead Market'

ackie: Jamaican fruit
quattie: small coin

(a) Hear recordings of calypsos/given Latin American dances. Accompany appropriately.
(b) Listen to the first ten minutes of Stravinsky's 'Rite of Spring'. The recording will give details of the 'programme'. Its ostinati and discords caused a riot at its first performance in 1913.
(c) Compare the first movements of Stravinsky's 'Dunbarton Oaks' and Bach's 3rd Brandenburg Concerto. Why is 'neo-Baroque' more appropriate than neo-classical?

This song has alternating bars of 6/8 and 3/4 time:
'Cancelling the fraction' changes the effect.

(d) First make yourself familiar with the story of this musical play/film (from record sleeve, etc.) It is based on Shakespeare's *Romeo and Juliet*—but in a modern American setting.
In the following excerpts, notice:
Prologue: Off-beat finger snaps (join in).
Dance at the Gym: Various dance rhythms. Try to identify them.
'Maria': Opening recitative. The final repeated 'Maria' modulating into the major for the song. A descending sequence beginning 'Say it loud'.
'America': Latin American rhythms, recitative and then the following song. This is repeated with more words, in alternation with another tune.
Quintet: An ensemble where the characters first sing solo, then combine in counterpoint.

A Song from *West Side Story*: 'America' — Leonard Bernstein

Things to do

12. Practise clapping page 73 rhythms (a) and (b) in alternation. Accompany 'America' playing them on alternate instruments/players. Discuss (i) how exactly bars 5–8 are a transposed version of 1–4, (ii) the key(s) of 5–8. Bars 1–4 each 'spell out' the chord required. Add a DIY accompaniment here.

Conducting and leading

Bernstein, besides being a composer, pianist and musical scholar, is also a famous conductor. Conductors have a difficult job. They decide the INTERPRETATION, rehearse and conduct the performance, controlling tempi and dynamics, usually using a baton:

Starting can be tricky, even with pieces beginning on a beat

Professional conductors often only give the previous beat:

When there is a half or quarter-beat anacrusis a gesture during the starting beat helps synchronise the start:

It may be safer with inexperienced conductors or performers to beat the entire preliminary bar. In quadruple time, just the second half of the bar should be enough to give the tempo and starting point.

Adapt to different beat units. Why is starting a race without a 'set' like having a bad conductor? What is an 'interpretation?

Today's ensembles

If a few singers gave you trouble, how would you control big groups? Many later composers require a larger orchestra than the classical one (page 18). Fortunately, conductors know where to look when bringing instruments in. This is the usual layout:

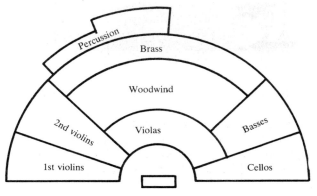

Things to do

13. Beat each time with accel and rall. Beat with (a) recordings, (b) 'Linstead Market'. Notice syncopation.

14. Discuss/practise conducting the starts of the songs on pages 8, 12, 29, 33, 36, 41, 47, 51, 73.

Occasionally, the second violins are opposite the first. Any extra instruments fit in where they can. The leader is also very important. He advises on bowing, and conducts when necessary.

At the last night of the Promenade Concerts, conductors even have to put up with a noisy audience—especially in the following.

👂(e) Listen to and conduct Elgar's *Pomp and Circumstance* March No. 1. Using A and B for its two main musical ideas, write down the plan. What words are associated with B? What are 'proms'? Name their founder and the hall used.

The instrumental line-ups of other ensembles have also become fairly established:

Brass bands

Most instruments are different-sized members of the saxhorn/flugelhorn families—a cross between the trumpet and the horn. A typical British line-up would include cornets, saxhorns, baritones, euphoniums, basses—as well as trombones and a bass drum.

Military (Concert/wind) bands

In these, the above might be joined by saxophones and orchestral woodwind/brass/percussion.

Jazz bands

These may be 'big bands' or small groups. Melody instruments vary, but include single 'reeds' (clarinets, alto/tenor/baritone saxophones) and 'brasses' (trumpets, cornets, trombones). The 'rhythm' section could be piano/banjo/guitar, vibraphone double bass and drum kit.

Pop and folk groups

The former usually employ metal strung amplified solid guitars (including bass), the latter favour acoustic guitars. Pop groups may also have drum kits, electronic keyboards, etc.

All ensembles need somebody to set the tempi. Large ones have a conductor. Small groups usually have a lead player/singer to do the job. In jazz, soloists also take turns leading as they improvise variations (BREAKS) on 'standard' tunes. The BLUES chords, associated with negro folk music, have been much used. For example:

$$\begin{vmatrix}4\\4\end{vmatrix}\ I\ |I\ |I\ |I\ |IV|IV|I\ |I\ |V\ |IV|I\ |I\ \|$$

A type of piano jazz, called BOOGIE WOOGIE, uses blues chords, tremolos and a syncopated RH over a LH dotted rhythm ostinato. RAGTIME was also once popular.

👂(f) Compare (e) on brass and military bands.

(g) Compare different jazz groups. Identify lead instruments in solo breaks.

(h) hear (i) boogie woogie, identifying chords I, IV and V, (ii) piano rags, (iii) 5/4 jazz.

Things to do

15. Identify the group/leader in pupil's pop/folk records. Owners must say why it is a favourite.
16. Match orchestra picture and plan on page 74. Compare the picture on page 18. Identify (a) leader's desks, (b) instruments in common, (c) additional instruments in the former.
17. Name the instruments in (a) the group opposite, (b) any local groups/bands.
18. Play the above blues progression in key C. Use DIY chords with boogie woogie piano.
19. Write what you can of 'Land of Hope and Glory' in D using instrumental help—or just your ear. Name the modulation.
20. Discuss the special problems when conducting marching bands/singing in big stadiums.

Assignments

(A) From newspapers, find out which musical shows are on locally and in London.
(B) List the instruments used by (a) the leader, (b) supporting artists in 'top twenty' groups.
(C) List/illustrate (a) famous orchestras, choirs and conductors, (b) ensembles chosen from those given. Use newspapers/*Radio Times*/record magazines.

17 MUSIC WITH EVERYTHING

Sound transmission

Conductors have another problem when bands play and march simultaneously, or when performers are spread over a big distance. Although sound waves travel through the air at about 750 mph (imagine a pond ripple travelling at this speed!).

The delay over longer distances is noticeable. Unless performers look at their conductor/leader, both music and marching can get out of step.

Sound (and water) waves behave rather like those jerked along a rope.

Despite appearances, each piece of rope (or water) does not really move along. It is more like a nudge passed quickly along a row of people. This type of vibration also occurs within the tube of a wind/brass instrument. However, whether they originally occur in a tube, wire, bar or vocal cord, they are quickly 'nudged' (not blown) through the air to the listener.

An interesting reverse process can also occur. When a silent string, bar or tube 'hears' its own fixed fundamental vibrating speed in the surrounding air, it vibrates in sympathy (RESONATES) (just as we tap our feet when we hear a tempo we like):

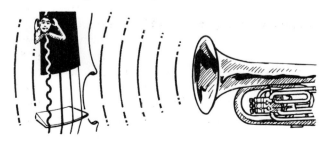

This helps us detect harmonics. Sympathetic RESONANCE can also occur in an instrument's bodywork. This both increases and improves the tone.

Things to do

1. Discuss lightning, echoes and the Concorde in relation to sound travel. Suggest why the pitch of sirens/trains/planes, etc. descends after they have passed by.
2. Jerk 'waves' along a rope on the floor. Now pass 'nudges' along a line of pupils. Which illustration best represents air waves?
3. Excite sympathetic resonance by placing a vibrating tuning fork on a window, drum, etc. Damp the resonance and compare the sound. Discuss (a) why church organs, etc. can make objects rattle, (b) why some singers can break glasses, (c) why soldiers break step when crossing a bridge, (d) why chime bars, glockenspiels, etc. are placed over tubes or boxes.
4. Identify the parts of stringed instruments, chime bars, xylophones, etc., that vibrate sympathetically. See if the tone is affected when this part is damped.
5. Sing a low note, feeling the resonance in your neck. Notice it go as the pitch rises. Now hear how a changed face/mouth shape or a hand in the mouth affects the tone of sustained sounds.
6. 'Undress' the piano and revise the names, function and action of its pedals and internal parts. Now, with all dampers off, hear the resonance as (a) a glissando is sung, (b) one pitch is sung.
7. Turn to the C harmonic series on page 68. Hear the sympathetic vibration as the fundamental is loudly played and the piano key of each harmonic is silently depressed in turn.
8. Place a small paper 'hook' on the open string of a horizontal violin, etc. Observe the vibration as (a) that note and (b) lower notes (of which it is a harmonic) are played on the piano. What do Activities 7 and 8 prove?

Performance and interpretation

The timbre/tone of an instrument is mainly determined by harmonics and the resonance of its body. Unlike others, stringed instruments seem to improve with age. Baroque violins by Stradivarius now fetch thousands of pounds!

However, players can always improve the tone.

With orchestral strings, both open string pitch and finger stopping must be accurate for good tuning (INTONATION). Also, when appropriate, a LH finger wobble (vibrato), enriches the tone.

Wind/brass intonation can often be finely controlled (a) by pulling tube joints in/out, (b) by changing embouchure or strength of breath.

As the oboe's pitch is difficult to adjust, other instruments tune to it. Wind players also have to cope with a slightly sharper pitch as their instrument (or the atmosphere) warms up.

String and brass players can also use MUTES to modify the vibrations (indicated CON SORDINI):

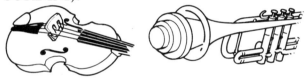

Like the piano una corda pedal, they soften the tone. Various shapes of mute (e.g. 'WA–WA') are used in jazz.

Performers/conductors should also INTERPRET each piece. The tempo, dynamics, phrasing, balance of parts, etc. must be musical. There can be good (and bad) interpretations.

Things to do

9. Discuss (a) the cost of class/personal instruments, (b) the meaning(s) of 'tone', 'a sharp', 'sharper than', (c) temperature and pitch.
10. Hear (a) string players demonstrate tuning, stopping, vibrato, mutes, (b) wind/brass players demonstrate mutes and fine tuning as described above, (c) pieces. Criticise (i) playing, (ii) interpretation.

In your notebook

(i) List the characteristics expected in high-quality instrumental/vocal performance.

(a) Rehear the Debussy Prelude (page 63). It begins with strings and horns respectively muted and unmuted. Detect when the mutes are later put off/on in these groups.
(b) Hear other orchestral/jazz pieces featuring muted strings/brass.

The way musicians perform can affect the mood of a piece. His choices of Instrument/Orchestration, Musical Material and Performing Method/Style decide the basic mood, just as they help illustrate programme music like the Debussy Prelude.

(c) Listen to twentieth-century Programme works. Guess each 'programme' suggesting which aspects of the above categories helped.
(d) Listen to the 2nd and 4th movements from Bartok's Concerto for Orchestra. Although not a normal concerto, most instruments have important solo spots:

Play of the Couples: Pairs of the wind instruments featured play at a constant interval apart. The five intervals are the clashing (major/minor) 2nds and 7ths, the pleasant (major/minor) 3rds and 6ths, and the oriental perfect 5ths. First hear rows of each interval on the piano. Discuss why inversions of any interval share the same 'flavour'. Now listen to the movement.

After side drum taps, identify each interval and instrument (one pair is muted). More drum taps introduce a Bach-like chorale on the brass (but with more modern harmony) followed by the first appearance of the horns. Finally, the couples return. Is the order as before? It ends as it began, with the side drum.

During a second hearing, concentrate on the string accompaniment to the 'couples'. Identify pizzicato, glissandi (slides), shakes, use of mutes and tremolos. Discuss its form.

Interrupted Intermezzo ('between piece'): In this, Bartok poked fun at a tune from Shostakovich's Seventh Symphony.

After a string phrase, listen to musical 'conversation' in the woodwind. Identify prominent instruments. After a Romantic string tune, the wind 'conversation' resumes! A string 'um pah' introduces the Shostakovich tune—immediately followed by 'laughter'. This is repeated.

After prominent percussion (triangle, cymbals and gong) the Romantic tune returns on muted strings. The movement ends with more wind 'conversation'. Hear the Shostakovich movement quoted. Discuss whether the laughter is deserved. Hear the 'laughter' in a different recording. Compare the interpretations.

Contemporary sounds

Recently, electronics, new instruments and unusual ways of playing old ones have given composers an even wider choice of musical effects. The new sounds are particularly used in contemporary, beat-less music.

Things to do

11. Take a chime bar and add a vibrato to the sound by moving a piece of card over the resonator hole. What has this to do with (a) violin playing, (b) jazz? Experiment to get other new sounds from pitched/unpitched instruments/objects. Now repeat Chapter 7 (16) (c) as before, (d) ignoring pitch indications and using your experimental pitched/unpitched sounds instead.
12. Perform, using the above experimental sounds:

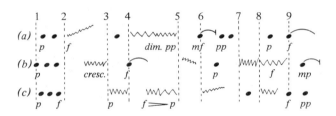

Is this an aleatory piece? Compose and perform similar pieces, each part being for one of the Bartok 'Couples' intervals. Invent new symbols for any new playing methods required.
13. Assemble a one-octave chime bar scale. Invent a system of 'change ringing'—repeating the descending scale with a different note out of place each time. Perform (a) solo, (b) with one player to a bar.
14. Play a simple tune on the above. Now swap the bars around and play as if you have not done so.
15. Tune bottles with water to make a scale when hit. Compare the pitches blowing across the tops. Repeat 13, and 14, but take off or add random amounts of water to make a microtonal scale. Will this remind you of bad violinists?

 (e) Listen to contemporary aleatory music. Try to note any unusual titles. Try to identify (a) instruments, (b) performing methods. Can you beat time with the music?
(f) Hear e.g. Indian microtonal music.

New uses of music

Music's power to create moods—or make you think of 'something else'—is much increased by these new sounds. This is now exploited in many ways. For example, most films, TV and radio programmes have introductory music/'signature tunes' to set their mood. Many also have background music. This matches what is happening, or makes you think of something you cannot see—like lurking danger. Similar devices appear in TV advertising music. The music used can be suitable old pieces, specially composed music or experimental sounds.

In the past there could only be 'live' music. Now, with radios, records and cassettes, we cannot get away from it. Consider the proportion of music in any *Radio Times*:

Things to do

16. Discuss (a) places, occasions and uses associated with music under (i) traditional, (ii) contemporary; (b) how music can persuade, stimulate, calm, create fear. Imagine a world without music. What things would be different?
17. Discuss the effectiveness of television advertising jingles/music. Is this an honest way to use music's power? Identify any 'classical' music used.
18. In groups, make up and perform television jingles for real or imaginary products.
19. Suggest instruments/musical ideas (see pages 60, 62) appropriate for:
(a) Advertising (i) a cooling drink, (ii) perfume, (iii) cereal, (iv) Caribbean holiday, (v) car.
(b) Films about (i) air battles, (ii) China, (iii) jungle, (iv) fairground, (v) Henry VIII, (vi) cowboys.
(c) Concert Programme Music illustrating (i) a railway journey, (ii) dawn, (iii) your teacher, (iv) an execution, (v) a drunk, (vi) you, (vii) fireworks.

Next time you are viewing a frightening television play/film with background music/sounds, (a) turn the volume down, (b) imagine pleasant music. Either way, notice less tension.

20. In any one day's radio and television schedule (all channels), compare the time devoted to programmes (a) purely of music, (b) using music, (c) without music. Which also have signature tunes? Sing/identify as many as you can.

(g) Hear recordings of television/radio signature tunes and film theme music. Identify or at least guess each mood/theme. Name any prominent instruments and suggest why they and the music are suitable. Where appropriate identify the composer and whether it was specially composed. For fun, imagine an obviously wrong programme/film as you listen!

The guitar and pop

The history of 'serious' music has been a story of many styles: so has the much shorter and quicker-changing history of pop music. The music scene now changes very rapidly. The following was very popular in the 1960s. I wonder if it will be remembered when you are sixty-four!

The guitar has been associated with pop/folk music for some time now. 'Serious' composers have also written for it this century. The different styles of guitar music (and playing) include CLASSICAL (SPANISH) and FLAMENCO.

'When I'm Sixty-four' Lennon and McCartney (The Beatles)

Things to do

21. In bars 1–8, hear how chromatic notes 'colour' the harmony. Where could phrasing slurs be put? Identify (a) its form, (b) cadences at bars 15/16, 30/31, (c) the key at bars 23/24, (d) syncopation.

22. Arrange it for available instruments. Take the song on page 73 as a rough model. Any cello/bass part can have fifths in long chords. Add a player hitting four objects on each of the four beats. Perform and record.

23. Discuss (a) your, (b) teacher's, (c) parent's present preferences in pop/folk 'classics', giving reasons. Have tastes changed? Must disliked music be bad (and vice versa)?

(h) Listen to a recording of the above song.
(i) Hear the first movement of *Concierto de Aranjuez* by Rodrigo (Spain). Is it 'conservative' or 'modern'?
(j) Compare solo guitar music in other styles.

Index

Capital letters indicate the first use of that technical term in the series. Terms already introduced in Books 1 and 2 are not generally shown.